# Transitioning Registered Handler- Animal Therapy from the Institution to the Community

## A Research Study

*Photo courtesy of Pet Partners*

**Analeah Green, Ph.D.**

Author:   **Analeah Green, B.A., M.S.W., Ph.D.**
Howard Beach, NY
analeah.green.phd@gmail.com

Publisher:   **Dawn D. Boyer, M.Ad.Ed., Ph.D.**
Virginia Beach, VA 23464
Dawn.Boyer@me.com

Copyright ©   2015
ISBN Numbers   **ISBN-13: 978-1511467971**
**ISBN-10: 1511467975**

**Disclaimer:**
The author has attempted to gather as much of the facts and information to the utmost complete and truthfulness for the compilation of this book from bona fide sources, internet sources, printed material in currently circulating and non-circulating sources, newspaper articles, personal interviews. Dates noted were from publically available sources.

Keep in mind – if any data included (or left out, incorrectly quoted, or attributed), it may be attributed to transcription errors or types. Several bodies of research were interpretations of the same or original documents and errors might have occurred as transcribed. Some material offered data that seemed to 'fit' or match other known and documented facts. Anyone with more data to contribute to a future, updated, and corrected version of this project is encouraged to send materials to email address noted above.

LinkedIn profile: www.linkedin.com/in/analeahgreen
Facebook Business Page: https://www.facebook.com/agreenphd

# Transitioning Registered Handler-Animal Therapy

# from the Institution to the Community

by

Analeah Green, Ph.D.

Ph.D. Walden University, 2013
Masters of Social Work, New York University, 2008
Bachelor of Art, State University of New York College,
Cortland, 2006

Dissertation Submitted in Partial Fulfillment
of the Requirements for the Degree of
Doctor of Philosophy
in

Human Services, Administration, and Leadership
Walden University

Dr. Barbara Benoliel, Committee Chairperson,
Dr. Jan Ivery, Committee Member
Dr. Amy Ford, University Reviewer
Human Services Faculty
Dr. Eric Riedel, Chief Academic Officer

This text has been altered in format from the original dissertation document to conform to easier to read for the general public and commercial publishing standards. Scholars reviewing the contents and formatting for standardization for thesis or dissertation should *not* use this book's current formatting as a model. Please see your school's guidelines for the acceptable formatting for the graduate level thesis researched.

# TABLE OF CONTENTS

## LIST OF TABLES

## LIST OF FIGURES

# ACKNOWLEDGEMENTS

I thank my friends and family, especially my husband, who supported and encouraged me throughout my doctoral education. I thank my dissertation committee members: my committee chair, Dr. Barbara Benoliel, and committee member, Dr. Jan Ivery for their expert guidance, knowledge, and overwhelming support of this topic. I would like to express my sincere gratitude to the registered handler-animal teams that participated in this study. I thank the coordinator of the therapy animal program, for your time, invaluable insight, and encouragement.  I thank the director of communication, for your time, involvement, and contributions to the book. I thank my canine companion, Rhino, for his company and constant reminder of my passion for this topic. Lastly, I thank the animal therapy community, for your dedication and efforts to advance the field.

Analeah Green, Ph.D.

*Analeah Green, Ph. D*

## ABSTRACT

**Transitioning Registered Handler-Animal Therapy**

**from the Institution to the Community**

**Analeah Green, Ph.D.**

**Walden University, 2013**

Across the nation, the older adult population has been growing in number. While traditional talk therapy services have been provided to these older adults through community-based organizations, minimal attention has been given to Animal-Assisted Therapy (AAT). AAT has primarily been utilized in institutional settings, leaving a gap in service delivery to older adults aging in communities. Guided by the human-companion, animal-bond conceptual framework and the theoretical frameworks of Gemeinschaft and Gesellschaft and mechanic and organic solidarity, survey data on attitudes and perceptions of 18 animal handlers for AAT and the concept of community care was explored using a qualitative, phenomenological research study design.

Data was analyzed using content analysis for themes to better understand the experiences of registered handlers. Lived experiences of registered handlers revealed emotional well-being of older adults require attention and could be addressed through administrative leadership and increased awareness of registered handler-animal therapy services. With study findings, case management agencies at the local and city level can consider integrating registered handler-animal therapy services into existing service care plans or establishing programs in under-developed case management agencies in hopes of meeting the needs of older adults who are aging in place.

# CHAPTER I

# INTRODUCTION

The older adult population in the United States has been growing dramatically. By the year 2030, researchers estimate individuals, ages 65 and older will double to 70 million (Masotti, Fick, Johnson-Masotti, & MacLeod, 2006). Oldest old adults, or individuals age 85 and over, are the fastest growing age group and are expected to reach 90 million by the year 2050 (United States Census Bureau, 2001). With the number of aging older adults significantly increasing and choosing to remain in their homes as they age (Scharlach, 2009b), there is a need for appropriate and effective community-based programs with services to meet a variety of physical and psychological needs. Generally, the physical needs of aging Americans have been met by existing city, state, and privately funded organizations (New York City Department for the Aging, 2012). While services, typically talk-therapy interventions, exist to address the psychological needs of older adults, minimal recognition has been given to the benefits of animal-assisted therapy (AAT) practices (Behling, Haefner, & Stowe, 2011; Risley-Curtiss, 2010).

This study was an exploration of the concept of community AAT and transitioning a therapy animal program in New York State from institutional to community-based settings. The need for this study was due to the rapidly growing older adult population, not only in New York State but nationwide (United States Census Bureau, 2001). The findings of this study explore the adaptation of animal-assisted therapy in New York State, thus minimizing the gap in knowledge in potential service delivery for the older adult population.

In this chapter, the researcher provided background of the topic, which was the foundation for the problem statement and the purpose of the study. The researcher provided research questions for this study as well as the conceptual and theoretical frameworks. Also discussed was the nature of the study, the definitions used, as well as the assumptions, limitations, and delimitations of the study. Lastly, the researcher discussed the significance of this study and provided an outline of proceeding chapters.

## Background

According to the New York City Department for the Aging (2012), the residents 60 years and over in Brooklyn and Queens accounted for 30% of the city's population, followed by Manhattan (21.3%), the Bronx (14.7%) and Staten Island (6.2%) indicating a demand for social, health care, and long-term care services to aide homebound older adults (New York City Department for the Aging, 2012). As such, community support services need to be prepared to provide comprehensive services to meet the emotional and psychological needs of aging individuals.

An intervention found to be effective and beneficial is animal-assisted therapy (AAT). Researchers have asserted the utilization of AAT among a variety of populations and in-patient environments showed positive outcomes and benefits. For aging individuals in nursing homes and hospitals, the use of AAT was shown to decrease anxiety and stress, while increasing socialization and cognitive functioning (Kramer, Friedmann, & Bernstein, 2009; Le Roux & Kemp, 2009; Williams & Jenkins, 2008). The problem was researchers had yet to explore animal-assisted therapy and its adaptations as potentially beneficial interventions at the community level. In New York State, the adaptation would be handler-animal therapy, with a handler trained by an organization, and an animal with no specific training. The researcher explored this adaptation in chapter three.

## Problem Statement

One of the challenges for the human services profession in New York State has been being knowledgeable of how to implement an adaptation of goal-oriented AAT in New York State in a community setting. Registered handler-animal therapy teams have volunteered services to institutional, in-patient facilities to alleviate the emotional and psychological distress experienced by the patient population. With a growing aging population residing in their homes and neighborhoods, there is an opportunity to provide this intervention in community-based locations, including but not limited to senior centers, adult day centers, and in the home, where many New York State older adults are present. Researchers have yet to explore how animal-assisted therapy practitioners regard the concept of community care. This lack of knowledge may be a barrier to providing community-based, animal-assisted therapy that could be investigated further.

## Role of the Handler

Representatives of the therapy animal program involved in this study train the individual (e.g., the registered handler) and it is the responsibility of the owner to train the animal. Following successful completion of a four-stage training/screening process for the person and animal, they are considered to be a registered handler-animal therapy team. The researcher discussed the training and screening process in detail in chapter three.

Upon receipt of an acceptance letter and identification tags for the registered handler and animal, the individual can arrange visits to facilities on a volunteer basis (no monetary compensation). Because the registered handler is not required to be a mental health professional versed in animal therapy techniques nor is the animal required to have undergone formal therapy training, registered handler-animal therapy sessions are supervised and monitored by a professional staff member of the facility. While patient-specific goals are outlined by the professional staff member, the registered handler-animal therapy team is an integral component of the treatment process as they acted as the catalyst for goal-oriented tasks (e.g., muscle movement, speech patterns). Moreover, without the registered handler there would not be a therapy animal.

The role of the registered handler is multi-faceted. Handlers are the owners and trainers of the therapy animal, they are liaisons between patient and health care professional, as well as emotional supports for patients and their families in times of crisis or grief. The perspectives and reports of the lived experiences as a registered handler have the potential to provide insight into transitioning this service into community-based environments. Community-based environments are not only preferred by the aging population to access supplemental services, but also where social workers, counselors, and case managers are employed, which is an opportunity to expand this volunteer-based service.

## Purpose of the Study

The purpose of this study was to explore the beliefs, experiences, perspectives, and observations of registered handler-animal therapy individuals who volunteered their services in New York State in relation to community-based AAT. Registered handlers, affiliated with one of the primary animal therapy programs in the United States, were selected for this study as this organization was referenced as one of the primary animal therapy programs throughout the United States. Registered handlers responded to open-ended questions created by the researcher to explore and better understand the following: reasons for using this intervention primarily in institutional (i.e. in-patient) settings, potential barriers in transitioning this intervention to community-based settings, and their willingness to volunteer in community-based locations. These concepts are stated in detail as the research questions for this study.

## Research Questions

Overall, this research study was guided by the following major exploratory research questions:

1. Which attributes of institutional settings (i.e. nursing homes, hospitals, rehabilitation facilities) assist in the utilization of registered handler-animal therapy practices?

2.  What barriers may exist in transitioning registered
    handler-animal therapy practices to community
    settings (i.e. in home services, senior centers,
    adult day care programs)?

3.  How willing are registered handlers to practice in
    community settings?

### Study Framework

The conceptual framework that guided this study
was the human-companion animal bond (Horowitz,
2008). According to the literature reviewed for this study,
the emotional connection a person has to his or her pet
can have positive emotional affects. Companion pets
have been researched to minimize loneliness and
depression, while increasing physical activity (Netting,
Wilson, & New, 1987).

The concept of the human-companion animal
bond indicated an association exists between emotional
well-being and the presence of an animal, which has
contributed to the establishment of animal-assisted
therapy practices. An extensive discussion regarding the
benefits and the varied applications of AAT, generally

practiced in institutional or in-patient environments, appears in chapter two.

While the benefits of AAT practices have been documented within an institutional setting, research has yet to be conducted at the community or out-patient level. However, there have been theoretical emphases on community and individual well-being. Tönnies (2001) discussed how the community (Gemeinschaft) evolves from being family-based to a developed society (Gesellschaft) as a result of an increase in business and trade. Similarly, Durkheim's (1947) theories of division of labor and organic solidarity demonstrate a person's ability to maintain independence, while maintaining societal connections. These theorists asserted the establishment and involvement of a community impacts the well-being of individuals, which is discussed and further demonstrated with contemporary examples of community models for older adults in chapter two.

The conceptual framework of the human-companion animal bond coupled with the theoretical frameworks on the concept of community were used to create the exploratory questionnaire to better understand the barriers of transitioning animal therapy practices to community settings. Tönnies (2001) and Durkheim (1947) recognized the complexity and importance of communities and the people who work within them. These theorists noted individual's skills impact how a community functions, thus providing means for prosperity and well-being (Putnam, 1993). This notion guided the overall nature of the study, which was to explore the practices of handlers and how registered handlers viewed community care.

## Nature of the Study

The selected approach for this study was a qualitative, phenomenological design. With a focus on obtaining perspectives, attitudes, beliefs, this approach allowed for exploration of the lived experiences as a registered handler providing animal therapy. Specific to New York State and following a thorough literature review, the participants for this study were individuals who were registered handlers through a nationwide organization that educates and trains people on the practice and use of animal therapy.

Utilizing the agency's website and publicly accessible database, the researcher retrieved contact information of individuals registered to provide animal therapy services. Following Institutional Review Board (IRB) approval and the informed consent process, an invitation to complete an electronic, open-format questionnaire was sent to the individuals' e-mail addresses. The questionnaire was accessible via www.surveymonkey.com where raw data were stored with anonymity to the survey respondents. Approximately six weeks following the call for participation, the researcher retrieved the data and transferred the metrics to spreadsheets for an extensive content analysis process and five follow-up telephone interviews. As described in chapter three, the researcher engaged in pre-coding and coding processes to identify themes and patterns. Prior to describing the data collection and data analysis process, the definitions pertinent to this study require consideration.

## Definitions

For the purpose of this study, the following concepts were defined:

*Animal-assisted therapy (AAT):* The formal, clinical education and training of the individual as well as the formal training of the animal in which the title AAT can be used (King, 2007). In New York State and under the reputation of the organization, any individual can complete the training course. Formal training of the animal is not required. In this way, the focus of this study was on registered handler-animal therapy. With the concepts that guided this study defined, the assumptions, limitations, and delimitations of the study required consideration.

Photo Courtesy of Pet Partners

*Community Setting:* An environment where individuals are considered out-patient. Out-patient status is flexible and services vary, based on individuals' needs (McCall, 2001).

*Institutional Setting:* For the purpose of this study, this term referred to a facility where individuals are given in-patient status. In-patient status is characterized as having 24-hour care, while living at a specific facility location.

*Registered Handler-Animal Therapy Team:* Individuals who volunteer time and their pet to visit in-patient facilities and provide handler-animal therapy. Working with a member of the treatment team in the facility, such as an occupational therapist, speech therapist, or medical professional, the registered handler works with a licensed professional to provide animal therapy in conjunction with other interventions to patients. In New York State, the nationally recognized organization trains the individual (the handler) and not the animal, as such it is recommended people who complete the training use the title registered handler-animal therapy team rather than AAT.

## Assumptions, Limitations and Delimitations of the Study

The findings of this study were intended to

increase knowledge and awareness among human service professionals on the impact of the human-companion animal bond and its potential importance within community-based services. The researcher was cautious in making generalizations from the findings. The limitations included the non-random and small sample size and the use of the exploratory questionnaire as the tool for research.

The non-random strategy and small sample size limited the generalizability of research findings as the recruited respondents were registered handlers, within a specific age range, and residing or volunteering in New York State. It is recommended additional research with heterogeneous and larger samples throughout the United States be conducted to allow a generalization of study findings.

The use of an open-ended questionnaire for the collection of data was a procedure allowing for only the exploration of perspectives and attitudes, intended to enhance understanding for evaluative purposes. The researcher did not assess the value, efficacy, or results of AAT in the community. Future research attempts may use pre-existing measurement tools as well as other exploratory strategies of inquiry to involve both quantitative and qualitative techniques to assert a more extensive strategy of evaluation. The use of this data collection tool required attention to concerns such as volunteer bias and response bias, which required steps to minimize these biases and enhance the integrity of questionnaire responses. Steps taken to address these concerns are discussed in detail in chapter three.

## Significance

The goal of this study was to inform human service professionals by providing insight and analysis of community-based AAT. Research findings identified barriers of transitioning registered handler-animal therapy services from the institution to the community, which can assist in program development and/or expansion to meet the needs of aging adults residing in the communities throughout New York State. Research findings assessed registered handlers were willing to volunteer in community-based settings; perhaps attention to the requirement of licensure and/or certification as a clinical professional is needed to promote the integrity and professionalism in the field of animal-assisted therapy. As such, this research study was designed to provide a foundation for future studies in an attempt to mobilize administration and leadership efforts within the human services profession.

## Summary

This study was an opportunity to explore the attitudes, beliefs, experiences, and perspectives of registered handler-animal therapy volunteers on transitioning this service from the institution to the community. In this interpretive approach, the researcher focused on the self-reported views, beliefs, assumptions, and first-hand experiences of the respondents. The research findings answered questions about the barriers associated with transitioning services from the institution to the community and the prospective willingness of volunteers to visit in community settings. The questions attempted to address the gap in knowledge regarding the benefits of animal therapy by producing data that were previously unavailable to determine whether such services would be valuable if practiced at the community level.

This study followed a qualitative, phenomenological design. Study findings were drawn from observed patterns, themes, or categories, based on the examination of the data gathered by an exploratory questionnaire. The focus targeted the respondents' phrasing in comments, how registered handler-animal therapy was described, as well as references and recommendations made by respondents regarding community-based settings. These procedures are discussed in detail in chapter three.

Chapters one and two of this study provided a synopsis of the growth of the population of older adults in New York State and the need for comprehensive community-based care. Also discussed were the benefits of AAT and its adaptation in New York State, known as registered handler-animal therapy. This descriptive information was used in the interpretation of the research findings to assess the integrity and insight provided by participants concerning what they believed were barriers of transitioning this intervention from the institution into the community. Participants' attitudes and beliefs were analyzed based on the conceptual framework of the human-companion animal bond and two theoretical frameworks focused on the integral involvement of a community and overall well-being of individuals. In chapter three, the researcher outlined the selected methodology of this study. The researcher described the study sample, data collection, and data analysis procedures. In chapters four and five, the researcher discussed the findings from the research study in detail as well as the social change implications.

Photo Courtesy of Pet Partners

# CHAPTER II

# REVIEW OF LITERATURE

## Introduction

Aging individuals and oldest old adults in particular are susceptible to chronic depression, attributable to recurrent losses of family members, friends, and physical abilities (Black, 2008). The psychological distress experienced by aging individuals should to be addressed to maintain their well-being and independence, as well as deter these individuals from pre-mature institutionalization (Masotti et al, 2006). Older adults have a strong desire to 'age in place' (stay in their own home for as long as possible before death), as there is a personal connection to the physical location where they grow old. The sense of attachment provides older adults comfort and stability in a stage of life where losses of various kinds are experienced (Scharlach, 2009b). As the older adult population and life expectancy increase, the number of older adults who age in place will climb, challenging community-based social service programs to meet emotional needs of clients.

An intervention that researchers have found to be effective and beneficial for older adults is animal-assisted therapy. Studies indicated the utilization of AAT among older adults in long-term care facilities showed a decrease in depression, anxiety, and aggression (Kawamura, Niiyama, & Niiyama, 2007; Le Roux & Kemp, 2009). Additionally, evidence showed facilities favored AAT programs for the psychological benefits of AAT sessions for patients (Behling et al., 2011). Prior to this study, researchers had not yet recognized animal-assisted therapy and its adaptations as beneficial interventions at the community level. In New York State, the adaptation has been handler (trained by an

organization)-animal (not trained) therapy, which the

researcher explored.

In this chapter, the researcher presented a

conceptual framework for examining the influence of

people's attachment to domesticated animals. The

researcher also presented two theoretical frameworks

that focused on community development and

contemporary examples of communities for older adults.

Also, discussed were issues of transitioning care to

community settings. Lastly discussed was the role of

registered handler-animal therapy teams, New York

State's version of animal-assisted therapy.

The following exploratory research questions

guided this study:

1. Which attributes of institutional settings (i.e.

   nursing homes, hospitals, rehabilitation facilities)

   assist in the utilization of registered handler-animal therapy practices?

2. What barriers may exist in transitioning registered handler-animal therapy practices to community settings (i.e. in home services, senior centers, adult day care programs)?

3. How willing are registered handlers to practice in community settings?

A review of literature on animal-assisted therapy guided this study. The books, journals, statistical reports, and electronic sources reviewed were sourced from the Internet, a local library, or obtained from a retail bookstore. The electronic databases included CINAHL Plus, EBSCOHost, LexisNexis, ProQuest, PsychINFO, SAGE, SocINDEX, and Google Scholar, which were searched for sources published between 2007 and 2011. The databases were accessed through Walden University Library. When using the selected search engine, the following key terms were used: *animal-*

*assisted therapy, canine therapy, pet therapy, age 85,*

*elderly, depression, anxiety, community, aging in place,*

*attitude,* and *animal therapy.* The key terms were used

to provide a foundational knowledge base of the

purpose, application, and effects of animal-assisted

therapy practices across the world. Key terms were also

used to identify that a gap in professional practice

existed in utilization of animal-assisted therapy practices.

Prior to implementing the research study, a

comprehensive literature review regarding animal-

assisted therapy was conducted.

## Animal-assisted Activities and Animal-assisted Therapy

It is important to distinguish the difference

between animal-assisted *activities* and animal-assisted

*therapy.* Animal-assisted activities are practiced by

professionals and volunteers with an animal. Animal-assisted activities consist of informal visits to an individual or a group of people where treatment goals are not specified, the volunteer and treatment provider does not track the person's progress, and the length of the visit with the animal varies (Le Roux & Kemp, 2009). In contrast, animal-assisted therapy is practiced by trained professionals, and the trained animal is a primary component in goal-oriented treatment. In this way, goals and objectives are identified and animal-assisted therapy sessions are customized to the person's individual needs. Additionally, animal-assisted therapy sessions are timed and the individual's progress is measured.

Animal-assisted therapy emerged in the 1980s, when psychologist Boris Levinson (as cited in King, 2007) included his dog into therapy sessions with non-communicative clients. Since then, animal-assisted therapy has been practiced in private or institutional settings including hospitals, hospices, in-patient/residential facilities, out-patient/rehabilitation practices, schools, camps, crisis intervention sites,

prisons, and animal shelters (King 2007; Kramer,

Friedman, & Bernstein, 2009). The purpose of animal-

assisted therapy is multifaceted and aims to improve

people's physical and mental health through motivational

and educational individualized sessions.

In studies where animal-assisted therapy was

used with hospitalized children, participants reported the

patient's perception of post-surgery pain to be reduced

(Tsai, Friedmann, & Thomas, 2010). Positive mood,

reduced stress, and lower anxiety were also found

among hospitalized children and adolescents when

engaged in animal-assisted therapy sessions. Tsai,

Friedmann, and Thomas (2010) asserted that positive

effects of animal-assisted therapy were expected to

increase in high-stress environments as sessions served

as an immediate form of distraction and stress relief,

especially among children.

For Friesen (2009), incorporating animal-assisted

therapy sessions in schools with children diagnosed with special needs reduced the frequency and severity of verbal and behavioral outbursts. Friesen's findings supported that the presence of a therapy dog provided a form of acceptance and support for the child. As a result of the positive connection with the dog, children became motivated to interact among classmates and adults (Friesen, 2009). Comparable effects of animal-assisted therapy have also been documented with adults diagnosed with a mental illness or form of substance dependence (Girt, et. al., 2009; Jasperson, 2010). The principles of animal-assisted therapy have also been researched using counseling theories.

Studies found the use of animal-assisted therapy within clinical practice built rapport with the client (patient), encouraged client (patient) involvement, as well as increased the emotional comfort for the individual (Chandler, Portrie-Bethke, Barrio Minton, Fernando, & O'Callaghan, 2010). In addition, individuals suffering from aphasia (disorder caused by damage to parts of the brain controlling language, making it hard to read, write, and say 'what you meant') reported animal-assisted therapy decreased stress levels and made the counseling session more enjoyable (Macauley, 2006). According to Wesley, Minatreat, and Watson (2009), therapy dogs can provide clients (patients) a form of physical touch while maintaining ethical boundaries within the working relationship.

The immediacy of animal-assisted therapy techniques coupled with the physical presence of a canine has proven in the last four decades to have positive effects on types of populations. For caregivers of individuals diagnosed with dementia, animal-assisted therapy decreased their anxiety and agitation from care-giving responsibilities (Connell, Janevic, Solway, & McLaughlin, 2007). Research supports animal-assisted therapy as a practical treatment option for professionals working with institutionalized individuals (King, 2007;

Kramer et al., 2009). With a growth in the aging population, institutional settings treating older adults are documenting similar outcomes when animal-assisted therapy is used.

## Institutional Settings of Older Adults
## and Use of Animal-assisted Therapy

Research has indicated depression is common among the oldest 'old adults' (age 85 and older) living alone or in an institution (hospital or nursing home) and can influence mortality (Cuijpers, Steunenberg, & Van Straten, 2007; Van der Weele, Gussekloo, De Waal, De Craen, & Van der Mast, 2008). However, the immediacy of animal assisted-therapy techniques has proven to alleviate grief and isolation, an aspect under-researched as an effective technique in treating depression among oldest old adults. In addition, individuals who touch and observe animals have shown to have a lower heart rate and blood pressure (King, 2007). Studies indicated individuals diagnosed with Alzheimer's or other forms of dementia had a decrease in anxiety and depression, as well as an increase in level of socialization when animal-assisted therapy was utilized (Kramer et al., 2009; Le Roux & Kemp, 2009). There is also a growing body of medical-based evidence supporting the calming effects of animal-assisted therapy (Williams & Jenkins, 2008). Animal-assisted therapy practices have also been explored from a program development standpoint.

## Implications for Professional Practice

Despite the growth in support of animal-assisted therapy programs, minimal program development has been made. From 1990 (13.7%) to 2010 (15.3%), there was only a 1.6% increase in the use of animal-assisted therapy programs in Illinois (Behling, et al., 2011). Behling, Haefner, and Stowe (2011) asserted that administrative concerns, coupled with being unfamiliar

with animal assisted therapy practices in general, limited

medical and social service professionals in this area.

Photo Courtesy of Pet Partners

Risley-Curtiss (2010) discussed the impact of

animals in a therapeutic environment has been under-

recognized in social work practice. The study consisted

of a random sample of 1,649 National Association of

Social Workers members. Participants completed (by

mail or online) a 38-question survey between June and

December 2005. Questions included exposure to

information/knowledge of animal-human relations;

inclusion of companion and other animals in assessment

and treatment; education and training; and

demographics. Data were analyzed using descriptive

statistics, specifically frequencies and means. Study

results indicated the majority of social workers did not

include companion animals in their assessment and

treatment of clients. In addition, 95.7% of participants

stated they did not receive any training or education on

animal-assisted therapy and social work practice (Risley-

Curtiss, 2010), further demonstrating a need for

additional research. To better evaluate the impact of

animal-assisted therapy practices, the conceptual

framework of the human-companion animal bond

requires consideration.

## Conceptual Framework

A growing body of literature has developed regarding the human-companion animal bond. Otherwise referred to as an individual's attachment to a companion animal or pet, the concept of the human-companion animal bond is grounded in social work practice. Researchers suggest the human-companion animal bond explores the person-environment concept and pet ownership demonstrates "physical, psychosocial, and economic dimensions" (Netting et al., 1987, p. 61). Human service professionals and researchers proposed the term *companion* invokes a nurturing, psychological connection enabling a strong attachment to form, thus contributing to positive effects (Beck & Katcher, 2003; Horowitz, 2008; Walsh, 2009).

Historically, cultures respected animals and attributed survival, health, and healing to their presence.

Animals were domesticated as humans transitioned from

a nomadic lifestyle to that of settlers, influencing the

progressive socialization of animals from servant to

companion (Walsh, 2009). Data from a national survey

indicated, as of 2009, approximately 63% of households

in the United States had at least one pet (Walsh, 2009).

Photo Courtesy of Pet Partners

Researchers also suggested the presence of a

human-companion animal bond can benefit an

individual's health by minimizing solitude and providing

emotional support (Netting et al., 1987; Risley-Curtiss,

Holley, & Wolf, 2006). Companion animals for older

adults provide a sense of purpose and self-worth, which

has been researched to decrease health risks, doctor

appointments, and overall health care costs (Horowitz,

2008; Walsh, 2009).

Attention to the human-companion animal bond

has led to the emergence of organized programs utilizing

animals in therapeutic interventions known as animal-

assisted therapy. Animal-assisted therapy programs and

their positive outcomes have been researched in

institutional settings, but have yet to be established at

the community level. Academic  and exploratory

research on the emotional impact of animals on

distressed individuals has the potential to bridge this gap

in knowledge for human service professionals. With an

increase in professional awareness, additional

opportunities to practice animal-assisted therapy and its

adaptations beyond an institutional setting are possible.

In order to identify the barriers associated with

transitioning this intervention from the institution to the

community, the notion of community-based care requires

exploration.

## An Overview of Community Level Care

Current community-based care options arose

from the Supreme Court's 1999 *Olmstead v. L.C. and*

*E.W.* decision. The Olmstead case involved two women

diagnosed with mental illness and retardation who were

institutionalized at a Georgia state facility. The women

requested treatment in their community of residence

once their medical conditions stabilized. In spite of the

agreement made with their team of professionals, the

women remained institutionalized (Yong, 2007). The

Supreme Court ruled this to be in violation of Title II of

the American Disabilities Act (ADA) that stated:

No qualified individual with a disability shall, by

reason of such disability, be excluded from

participation in or be denied the benefits of the

services, programs, or activities of public entity, or

be subjected to discrimination by any such entity

(42 U.S.C. § 12132 as cited by Yong, 2007).

The Olmstead decision prompted states to issue

and abide by new guidelines involving the use of

community-based services for all individuals with

disabilities (Kane & Cutler, 2009; Yong, 2007). For the

aging population, this ruling heavily influenced states to

reduce the occupancy rate in nursing facilities by

improving community-based services by creating

waivers, grant opportunities, and efforts to establish a

system of service delivery where the individuals live

(Lockhart, Giles-Sims, & Klopfenstein, 2009; Yong,

2007).

## Concept of Community Care for Older Adults

The Older Americans Act was passed by Congress (1965) marking the first political recognition that the older adult population was growing and in need of services. The legislation created grants for states to be used for community-based social services, staff development, and research (Older Americans Act (OAA) of 1965, Pub. L. No. 109-365, § 1). With substantial funding from the OAA, 33 states allocated funds to community-based services (Hudson, 2010). At the national level, 65% of public funds covered medical and/or personal care needs of individuals living in their homes (Lockhart et al., 2009).

For Yarmo-Roberts et al (2010), the aim of community-based service initiatives is to delay the individual's decline in health. According to Tang and Pickard (2008), "appropriate use of in home and community-based services was related to delaying

nursing home placement, reversing deterioration of

physical functioning, and increasing survival" (p. 405).

The notion of community-based care is to provide a

comprehensive level of services to aging individuals.

Services are provided by an array of non-professional

and professional staff including nurses, physical

therapists, social workers, and counselors (Stevenson,

McRae, & Mughal, 2008). The foundational objectives of

service provision in the environment of residence,

maintaining independence, considering each need

(medical, emotional, physical) of the older adult, and

fostering a community presence (Dallaire, McCubbin,

Carpenter, & Clement, 2008) are vital in community-

based practice.

Another purpose of community-based care is to

provide support to informal caregivers, such as family

members, friends, and neighbors (Wilson et al, 2008).

Results gathered from a retrospective study using

longitudinal data from the Health and Retirement Study

indicated that informal caregivers provided over 52 hours

a week of care to an older adult living in the community

(Rhee, Degenholz, Lo Sasso, & Emanuel, 2009). From

an economic standpoint, an informal caregiver provided

a range of approximately $22,514 to $42,351 of services

annually to aging individuals in 2002 (Rhee, Degenholz,

Lo Sasso, & Emanuel, 2009). Moreover, research

supports that older adults prefer to stay in their homes,

thus limiting the options for informal caregivers (Lehning

& Austin, 2010). As such, policy makers support

community-based services as a cost-effective approach

for meeting the needs of an aging population that

facilitate aging in place (Lehning & Austin, 2010). One

community-based model researched and proven to be

effective is the Program of All-Inclusive Care for the

Elderly (PACE).

## PACE: An Exemplar of Community-based Care

The PACE model emerged in the 1970s in San Francisco, California through a nonprofit agency OnLok Senior Health Services (Hansen, 2008; *National PACE Association*, 2002). OnLok, a Cantonese term for peace, was the vision for this community-based care system (*National PACE Association*, 2002). PACE consists of an inter-disciplinary staff to provide a range of services including

... primary care, specialty care, adult day care, home care, hospital care, nursing home care, medication oversight, and transportation to medical appointments. The primary site of delivery for many of the services is an adult day health care center ... each PACE center includes at least one physician, nurse, social worker, dietician, occupational therapist, physical therapist, and recreational therapist.

Complementing these professionals are home care

workers and other ancillary personnel, such as

drivers. (Hansen, 2008, p. 84)

Photo courtesy of Pet Partners

In regards to caregiver support, PACE offers a

variety of care coordination services. According to Yong

(2007), the care coordination process involves

knowledge, facilitation, and referrals for services within a

complex system of care. The PACE model demonstrates

this notion through case management, respite,

counseling, direct care as well as linkages to additional

service providers (Hansen, 2008) in order to alleviate

care giving responsibilities.

The unique and highly comprehensive PACE

model is established in 22 states and serves 15,000

people (Hansen, 2008). While beneficial to aging

individuals and their families, the PACE program is

extremely structured and regulated by state and federal

guidelines (Hansen, 2008), thus limiting the ability to

replicate this model to its fullest extent. Of the eight

locations in New York State, only two programs are

located in the metropolitan area (*National PACE*

*Association*, "Where is PACE," 2002). In spite of this

limitation, alternative forms of the PACE model, including

Naturally Occurring Retirement Communities, aging in

place, and aging friendly programs have emerged in the

New York metropolitan area to address the growing

older adult population. These community-based models

provide a range of services that vary from agency to

agency. Exploring the aspects of community care as

perceived by registered handlers could provide insight

on how to implement community-based AAT. Prior to

exploring the components of these community models, it

is imperative to understand the impact a community has

on one's livelihood from two theoretical standpoints.

## Theoretical Frameworks: Tönnies and Durkheim

## Tönnies' Gemeinschaft and Gesellschaft

During the industrial revolution, Tönnies (2001)

explored how the community evolved from being family-

based to a developed society as a result of an increase

in business and trade. Exemplified and maintained

through family, common beliefs and practices,

*Gemeinschaft* is an intimate form of community (Haidt &

Graham, 2009; Kamenka, 1965). In contrast,

*Gesellschaft,* or society references a weakness in

community bonds enabling individuals to pursue their own ambitions (Haidt & Graham, 2009).

For Tönnies (2001), a group of people in *Gemeinschaft* live harmoniously and share material possessions since strong interpersonal relationships are the origin of authority. According to Tönnies (2001), "Community ... requires and cultivates in its prominent citizens, who act as continual role models, as art of leadership and of overall living together" (p. 175). The traditional form of leadership fosters allegiance and respect among community members as *Gemeinschaft* law applies to the social whole (Mellow, 2005; Haidt & Graham, 2009). *Gemeinschaft* upheld common beliefs as well as common occupations including, "...brotherhoods of the arts and crafts, the communities and guilds, fraternities and ecclesiastical orders" (Tönnies, 2001, p. 204). In this way, the model of *Gemeinschaft* succeeded in rural areas.

As people transitioned to urban areas, law

directed management and government outweighed the
influence of traditional leadership. Shared experiences
and close relationships were replaced by business
associations, indicative of *Gesellschaft* (Tönnies, 2001).
*Gesellschaft* allowed individuals to pursue their own
ambitions – utilizing a commercial center for art, science,
and capital to increase prosperity. Essentially,
*Gemeinschaft* was replaced by commercial and financial
options, which weakened or eliminated interpersonal
relationships (Kamenka, 1965; Mellow, 2005). Kamenka
(1965) asserts an individual within Gesellschaft is
isolated so wealth and autonomy can thrive. Durkehim
also discusses the concept of autonomy.

## Emile Durkheim's Mechanical and Organic Solidarity

Durkheim recognized the community advanced
from a simplistic to a multi-faceted form as the industrial
age progressed and new machinery emerged. Thus,

Durkheim's division of labor theory and the role of the

individual also evolved. According to Durkheim (1947),

"Solidarity, which comes from likenesses, is at its

maximum when the collective conscience completely

envelope our whole conscience and coincides in all

points with it" as "individuality is nil" (p.130). Mechanical

solidarity linked the individual to society as social norms

were created and maintained within the group.

Norms established by the group enable

individuals to learn about appropriate relationships

resulting in conformity. Recognition of norms consists of

daily activities and provides individuals a purpose within

the community (Durkheim, 1961; Prus, 2009).

Mechanical solidarity also accentuates group integration

encouraging members to work towards a common goal

(Haidt & Graham, 2009). Homogenous groups indicative

of rural societies exemplify mechanical solidarity as " ...

each family forms a compact mass, and all devote

themselves to the same occupation" (Durkheim, 1947, p.

284). The division of labor is minimized and the collective life is maintained by common traditions and routines.

Mechanical solidarity has been characterized as being dependent on the social system as a whole. For Durkheim (1947), when members of a community execute similar responsibilities as all others in a community, the community maintains existence even when individuals die. Durkheim (1965) compared mechanical solidarity to that of "bonds of blood," and tradition (p. 432). In contrast, organic solidarity enabled an individual to be autonomous from society resulting in a complex division of labor. Specialization of tasks emerged as population size and diversity increased (Durkheim, 1947).

Organic solidarity portrays a society where social differentiation is prominent (Dew, 2007). Though individuals carry out different tasks and maintain different ideals, the order and continued existence of society depends on individuals performing their specific

tasks. This is seen particularly in complex societies

where individuals can specialize in a task thus allowing

for independence from the group. Although homogeneity

once maintained societal cohesion, differentiation of

tasks has a similar result. Viewed as a system of human

parts working together as a system, organic solidarity

maintains societal cohesion through this continuous

relationship. For Durkheim (1947), "Each part of the

animal, having become an organ, has its proper sphere

of action where it moves independently without imposing

itself upon others" (p. 192). In this way, autonomy exists.

Durkheim (1947) continues that in order for organs to

survive, "they should come together" (p. 365) thus

cultivating solidarity, a sense of community and

collective well-being otherwise termed as social capital

(Cannuscio, Block, & Kawachi, 2003).

## Community and Social Capital

For Putnam (1993), social capital is characterized by aspects of a social organization that maximizes coordination of services and cooperation of individuals for mutual benefit. The mutual benefit or collectivity aspect of social capital is distinct in that an individual who lacks strong social ties and support at a personal level can still benefit, physically and emotionally from living in a community with strong social connections (Cannuscio, Block, & Kawachi, 2003). Researchers have explored two types of social capital: bonding and bridging (Hawkins & Maurer, 2012; Collum, 2008; Keating & Dosman, 2009) that require discussion.

Bonding social capital is indicative of strong social ties among group members, typically an intimate, familial group providing emotional support. With bonding social capital, there is a dynamic of reciprocation in which one member provides assistance to an individual who previously provided help. In contrast, bridging social capital is characteristic of weak social and emotional ties in order to connect to a social organization to access communal resources (Hawkins & Maurer, 2012; Collum, 2008; Keating & Dosman, 2009). In spite of these differentiations, bonding and bridging social capital foster trust and engagement among members. Moreover, with an increase in the number of aging Americans and a shift in the traditional construct of a nuclear family unit, the need for social capital remains (Cannuscio, Block, & Kawachi, 2003). The concepts of community and social capital continue to exist in contemporary society, particularly for older adults.

## Theoretical Connection to Study

In response to the growing aging population, communities known as naturally occurring retirement communities (NORCs), aging in place, and aging friendly

were established in suburban and rural areas (Pynoos,

Caraviello, & Cicero, 2009; Scharlach, 2009a). These

communities provide a range of services including

medical, social, and nutritional programs (Castle,

Ferguson, & Schulz, 2009).

The NORC model, in particular upholds

communal ties by providing assistance to older adults,

indicative of Tönnies concept of *Gemeinschaft* and

bonding social capital. The availability of services in

home and on-site, executed by professionals of various

working backgrounds as well as volunteers, encourages

the autonomy of the individual and the success of the

program as a whole. This notion resembles Durkheim's

concept of division of labor and organic solidarity and

demonstrates the concept of social capital. Tönnies and

Durkheim recognized the unique dynamic between the

individual and society. Decades later, the concepts

continue to be applicable. Regardless of demographic

changes, the need for community will remain. Whether a community is constructed as the demand arises, or it is created following the natural aging process, a community and the services it provides enable individuals to be comfortable and safe in their homes. Aging in place is rapidly becoming a defining characteristic of an aging America and continual improvement of these community programs will assist in meeting the emotional needs of older adults and continuing the notion of social capital. In addition, Wood, Giles-Corti, and Bulsara (2005), asserted pet ownership is arguably a form of social capital as it is a means to facilitate social engagement, rapport building, and interaction. As such, exploring the motivating factors of handlers (pet owners) to practice in community-based environments could provide insight into how their services could be incorporated into service delivery plans for aging adults. Lastly, human service professionals who are familiar with aging in place communities have the potential to create an animal-

assisted therapy program within the existing model of

care.

Each older adult community model is slightly

different in construction, but each strive to provide older

adults, age 60 and older, the ability to remain in one

environment throughout the aging process to promote

independence, wellness, and safety (Castle, Ferguson,

& Schulz, 2009). The term naturally occurring retirement

communities (NORC), first used by professor Michael

Hunt in the mid 1980s, describes an unintentional

housing development for the elderly. Hunt discovered

over 50% of residents in United States cities were

elderly. Hunt encouraged cities to approach the "…

unintentional concentration of elders…" by creating

supportive services for an "… intentional community of

elders…" (Bookman, 2008, pp. 423-424).

Naturally occurring retirement communities

provide comprehensive services to residents (Scharlach,

2009a). Typical of urban environments in which the community is comprised of several buildings, services including case management, mental health care, medical and nursing services, and nutritional services are provided (Black, 2008). While NORCs are valuable service providers, a dense cluster of elders residing in one geographical area confined by infrastructure in suburban or rural areas is rare. As such, aging in place models have emerged.

The term aging in place refers to individuals remaining in their homes as they age, focusing on home modification to minimize barriers as result of physical disabilities (Alley, Liebig, Pynoos, Banerjee, & Choi, 2007). Known as home modification tasks, such as removing loose area rugs or installing handle-bars in bathrooms so the risk of falling is deterred. More complex modification projects include widening doorframes, in the event a wheelchair needs to be used or installing a ramp at front and back entryways (Pynoos,

Caraviello, & Cicero, 2009). Home modification enables the older adult to navigate within and outside the home, promoting the individual's independence and ability to engage in activities.

Aging in place allows elders to remain in their homes as they age, but also provides an approach to service delivery that eliminates an institutional setting. Elders who are aging in place can be referred to agencies that provide services to the older adult population. Once a connection is made, the older adult participates in an in-home assessment with a staff member. Upon assessment, an individualized service plan is created to address the needs of the older adult (Bookman, 2008). Services like home-delivered meals, housekeeping, homecare, transportation or caregiver respite could be provided. These services fall under case management programs that oversee multiple service providers. As elders remain in the home, formal services are delivered and social contact is maintained

(Everingham, Petriwskyj, Warburton, Cuthill & Barlett,

2009). It is important, however, to indicate that such

services are appropriate for older adults in need of

minimal help to live independently in their home. For

elders who require more comprehensive services, aging

friendly communities are more appropriate.

Aging friendly communities provide service

delivery across the lifespan, so if desired, the older adult

can reside in one location his/her entire life (Scharlach,

2009b). Aging friendly communities provide services in

three ways: in the home of the older adult, in ambulatory

care settings, and in formal institutions (Castle, et al,

2009). The integration of services "… is likely to improve

efficiency and quality of care, but it is also important

because it can reduce stress and frustration for elders"

(Castle, et al, 2009, p. 48). In-home services are similar

to the case management providers of aging in place

communities. Providing services in ambulatory settings

or medical care services that do not require hospital

admission provides elders opportunities to complete necessary medical examinations, like blood tests or x-rays.

The third form of service delivery provided by aging friendly communities is in institutional settings, usually in adult daycare centers, of which there are three forms. Adult day healthcare centers provide personal health through social interaction and medical related care. Adult day social care centers, commonly known as senior centers, provide a setting for leisure activities, trips, meals, and some health services. Adult daycare centers focus on older adults with a type of dementia or Alzheimer's disease. These centers provide medical related care as well as individual and social activities aimed to stimulate the elder's cognition and provide respite for the caregiver.

Naturally occurring retirement communities, aging in place and aging friendly communities provide concrete resources for older adults to aid them in living independently in their home. The physical and

nutritional needs of older adults are being met by these

valuable programs. The social and emotional distress

experienced by elders in the community could be

additionally addressed by implementing animal-assisted

therapy (AAT) practices. Ideally, access of New York

State's adaptation of animal-assisted therapy, known as

handler-animal therapy would be by referral through a

case management agency. Case management agencies

funded by New York City's Department for the Aging

(DFTA) offer a range of concrete services in each

borough. Services such as case management, caregiver

respite, and a senior center facility, home delivered

meals, homecare and housekeeping, and service

referrals for legal assistance and applying for Medicaid

are subsidized by the city of New York to little or no cost

to clients. In this way, individuals may pay a minimal

contribution for handler-animal therapy interventions

depending on their financial status. Similar to the

traditional naturally occurring retirement community model, community animal-assisted therapy services could be provided within the location of residence so aging individuals could access the service (i.e. local senior or adult day care center) with minimal burden. For homebound aging individuals, community animal-assisted therapy could be provided in home upon request and with documented permission by the individual, designated family members, and agency administrators. To better understand if this is feasible, an evaluation of barriers associated with services provided at the community level is required.

## Barriers of Community-based Care

Barriers of community-based care exist on a conceptual and organizational standpoint. The concept of 'ageism,' or the unconstructive outlook on the aging process, is prevalent in Western societies (Dallaire et al.,

2008). Social expectations surrounding the current aging population are vastly different from their peers several decades ago. The impact of longer employment, delayed retirement, marital status (i.e. divorce and widowhood), and extended livelihood of both genders strays from the assumption that old age equates to immediate institutionalization (Hudson, 2010). Contradicting norms and expectations towards the general aging population in the United States have resulted in discriminatory actions when services are required by older adults to maintain independence in the community (Dallaire et al., 2008; Hudson, 2010). Coupled with this stereotype is the complicated infrastructure indicative of community-based care systems.

For Nancarrow, Moran and Parker (2009) the existing model of community-based services involves a matrix of individual needs, resulting in a hierarchy of care ranging from low-level needs (community-based services) to high-level needs (hospital or rehabilitation services). This model of care involves a variety of

assessment and eligibility procedures, which has the

potential to affect the quality of care or delay receipt of

services (Lockhart et al., 2009; Hudson, 2010).

Resistance of family members also affects assessment

and eligibility procedures. Research supports that

requesting external support is a negative reflection of the

composition of the family. As such, support of an aging

individual is the responsibility of family and friends

(Hudson, 2010). For elders who would welcome

community-based supportive services, a barrier that

exists is the lack of awareness.

Research supports that community-based

supportive services are underutilized, primarily due to

the older adult population being unaware of the service

delivery system (Dallaire et al., 2008; Kane & Cutler,

2009; Tang & Pickard, 2008). Moreover, 44% of

participants (N=4,611) from the Community Partnership

for Older Adult Programs Survey, reported a lack of

knowledge surrounding their needs while aging in place

(Tang & Pickard, 2008). The obstacles associated with

navigating a multi-faceted community-based care

system without appropriate guidance results in a severe

loss of time, money, and use of much needed services

(Yong, 2009). Research indicates successful navigation

of services is dependent upon one's level of need and

geographical location in which programs may or not be

available in metropolitan and rural areas (Nancarrow,

Moran, & Parker, 2009; Yarmo, et al., 2010). The

difficulty in accessing services is magnified by the

shortage of professionals.

The insufficient number of professionals to meet

the needs of the growing older adult population is a

considerable concern. According to Lehnig and Austin

(2010), "... only 1% of physicians specialize in geriatrics

... 4% of social workers and less than 1% of nurses,

physician assistants, and pharmacists have received

training in geriatrics" (p. 46). Of the current workforce,

quantitative and qualitative data exists that identify

factors related to community-based work that deters

professionals from entering this field (Stevenson,

McRae, & Mughal, 2008). In a focus group study

conducted by Stevenson, MaRae, and Mugal (2008) the

experiences of community home health workers were

explored (N=39). Results indicated that home

environmental issues, poor communication with service

providers and client, entering high crime rate and drug

trafficking neighborhoods to conduct assessments, and

working alone were common risks as a community

based professional (Stevenson, McRae, & Mugal, 2008).

The findings of this study demonstrated that special

attention is needed to foster staff involvement, enhance

partnerships with agencies and other community entities

to provide a holistic system of care for the worker and

client, improve accountability practices, and pursue a

variety of local, state, federal, and private funding to

provide services to a growing older adult population

(Stevenson, McRae, & Mughal, 2008; Salau, Rumbold, & Young, 2007; Wilson, et al., 2008; Lehning & Austin, 2010). To better understand these factors and their association to the implementation of animal-assisted therapy practices in the community, the role of the individual required consideration. The problem is research on animal-assisted therapy professionals practicing in community settings is non-existent. To bridge this gap in knowledge, the role of the therapist from an occupational, art, and music therapy standpoint should be explored within a community context. These practitioners were chosen for review as they are under-recognized as trained individuals who execute beneficial therapeutic interventions, similar to individuals who practice animal-assisted therapy interventions. Through a review of literature, it will be explored the role of the therapist in community-based care is vital for the emotional and psychological well-being of clients (patients).

## The Role of Therapists in the Community

### Occupational Therapists

Occupational Therapy (OT) is described as a profession that assists individuals of all ages to accomplish physical goals through the therapeutic use of daily activities (*The American Occupational Therapy Association, Inc*, "About Occupational Therapy," 2012). The activities facilitate the relationship between the occupational therapist (OT) and client, resulting in an interactive and evolving treatment plan as goals are met, boundaries are set, and additional strategies are utilized (Holmqvist, Kamwendo, & Ivarsson, 2009). From a community-based standpoint, occupational therapists (OT) work with older adults on fall prevention (use of cane / walker) while living with chronic conditions such as diabetes, arthritis, and cardiac conditions (Quick,

Harman, Morgan, & Stagnitti, 2010). Through

collaboration with formal and informal supports, the OT

creates a supportive and reflective intervention that

identifies client strengths and weaknesses assisting in

the motivational attitude of the working relationship

(Graves, 2007; Holmqvist, Kamwendo, & Ivarsson,

2009). In addition, an OTs scope of practice is varied. It

is client specific which contributes to their ability to

assess and adapt efficiently (McCluskey & Middleton,

2010; Quick, Harman, Morgan, & Stagnitti, 2010).

Indications of the success of an occupational therapist

includes an understanding of human relations and the

complexity of the work as a balance between facilitating

activities and therapy goals (Graves, 2007; Holmqvist,

Kamwendo, & Ivarsson, 2009). This is also indicative of

art therapy professionals.

Photo Courtesy of Pet Partners

## Art Therapists

Art therapy has been utilized in the United States

and the United Kingdom since the 1940s. A type of

psychotherapy, art therapy uses creative processes that

are facilitated by a licensed professional who underwent

clinical training (Sweeney, 2009; Kelly, 2010; *American

Art Therapy Association*, "Art Therapy," 2012). This

intervention is considered to be an effective approach

across the lifespan in order to ascertain, explore,

comprehend and address psychological concerns

(Sweeney, 2009). The art making process engages the

client, which also creates a form of control allowing the

client to explore his or her concerns in a safe

environment. Group and individual art sessions have

been shown to progress emotional well-being and can

be found in community outreach programs (*American Art*

*Therapy Association*, "Art Therapy: Definition of the

Profession," 2012). Art therapists in the community often

work with issues related to anxiety, depression, grief,

loss, emotional, and physical abuse (Sweeney, 2009).

The benefits of art therapy have been researched;

however, professional art therapy positions as a mean of

gainful employment are limited. As a result, art therapy

positions are limited and gainful employment is difficult

to obtain in this field. Other mental health professionals

including social workers, counselors, psychiatrists, and

psychologists, are encouraged to use art therapy

professionals in conjunction to traditional talk therapy

practices (Kelly, 2010). Utilizing music therapists within

talk therapy practices has also been researched.

## Music Therapists

Music therapy is a therapeutic intervention using

music to obtain individualized treatment goals.

Introduced in the 1800s, and formalized in 1950 by the

National Association for Music Therapy (NAMT) followed

by the American Association for Music Therapy (AAMT)

in 1971, the music therapy profession was established

(*American Music Therapy Association*, "History of Music

Therapy," 2011). Facilitated by a credentialed music

therapist, music therapy has been shown to improve

physical movement, cognitive awareness, social

engagement, and emotional well-being throughout the

lifespan (*American Music Therapy Association*, "What is

Music Therapy?" 2011). For Gonzalez (2011), music

therapists undergo rigorous musical training prior to completing a music therapy program. In this way, the importance of self-awareness as a therapist and the creative abilities as a musician interplay in practice, resulting in a unique intervention. Research asserts that improvisation techniques using a variety of rhythms and tones of music have assisted individuals in recognizing their musical talents as well as providing an outlet for emotional expression (Gonzalez, 2011). Music therapists are employed by intermediate care facilities, including adult day care and senior centers, and provide in home care if contracted by a local agency or caregiver (*American Music Therapy Association*, 2011, "American Association for Music Therapy"). From a community-based context, music therapists are aware that individuals receiving services cope with a variety of health conditions. Termed as a "… whole health-care continuum …" (O'Grady & McFerren, 2007), music therapists are flexible in practice and readily adapt to the home environment altering the length and context of the session as needed. Older adults suffering from dementia or Alzheimer's showed a decrease in anxiety when music therapy was used and an increase in social interaction between the older adult and caregiver was reported (*American Music Therapy Association*, 2011, "American Association for Music Therapy"). Such results have also been documented when animal-assisted therapy was used.

## Connection to Animal-Assisted Therapy and Summary

The professional fields of occupational, art, and music therapy are similar to that of animal-assisted therapy. Each specialty utilizes a tool incorporated into the intervention plan. It is a concrete item to enhance daily living in occupational therapy, a creative tool used in art and music therapy, or a canine in animal-assisted therapy, thus the 'tool' is facilitated by a trained individual. Furthermore, the 'tool' is used to create a positive working rapport with the client enabling the individual to explore and address emotional and psychological distress. Literature supports that delineating from, or working in conjunction with, talk therapy practices with an under-recognized approach, like occupational, art, or music therapy, can benefit individuals of all ages and health conditions. Also demonstrated by the literature, the role of the trained individual is vital in a beneficial therapeutic intervention. However, animal-assisted therapy professional insights are non-existent. Unlike occupational, art, and music therapy, which have emerged in community-based settings, animal-assisted therapy practices have not. In an effort to bridge this gap in knowledge, the researcher executed a qualitative phenomenological study. Focusing on New York State's adaptation of animal-assisted therapy, the researcher strived to ascertain the barriers of transitioning registered handler-animal

therapy interventions from the institution into the

community.

## Method Review and Conclusion

Qualitative inquiry seeks to learn about a problem

or issue that participants are experiencing. The

researcher is an active participant throughout qualitative

inquiry as data can be obtained through interviews,

observations, or document review pertinent to study

participants. Information is then organized by themes

and interpreted by the researcher (Creswell, 2009). For

Creswell (2009), there are five approaches to qualitative

research: narrative, phenomenology, ethnography, case

study, and grounded theory. For the purpose of this

dissertation, phenomenological research emerged as the

most appropriate approach as it allows the perspectives

and lived experiences of New York State's registered

handler-animal therapy individuals to be at the forefront.

For Creswell (2009), phenomenological research explores a human experience as identified by study participants. It is a strategy of inquiry that involves an in depth approach and a relatively small study sample in order to better understand the area of focus. Another viable option was to utilize a case study approach that explores a program or event within a system. Since the focus of this research study is to gain insight from the perspectives, beliefs, and attitudes regarding the lived experiences as a registered handler providing animal therapy and not the program itself, a phenomenological approach was the most appropriate.

The sample for this study was a maximum of 20 registered handler-animal therapy teams. Contact information is publicly available through the agency website. The literature review conducted cited this organization to be the leading animal therapy association in the United States. Numerous affiliates throughout the country have partnered with them to train

and register individuals. The measurement tools

included an exploratory questionnaire created and via

follow-up telephone interviews. Prior to distributing the

questionnaire via www.surveymonkey.com, consent

forms for study participants were created. Study

objectives were approved by the Institutional Review

Board (IRB). The researcher provided details and steps

of the chosen methodology and discussed validity and

reliability concerns in the next chapter.

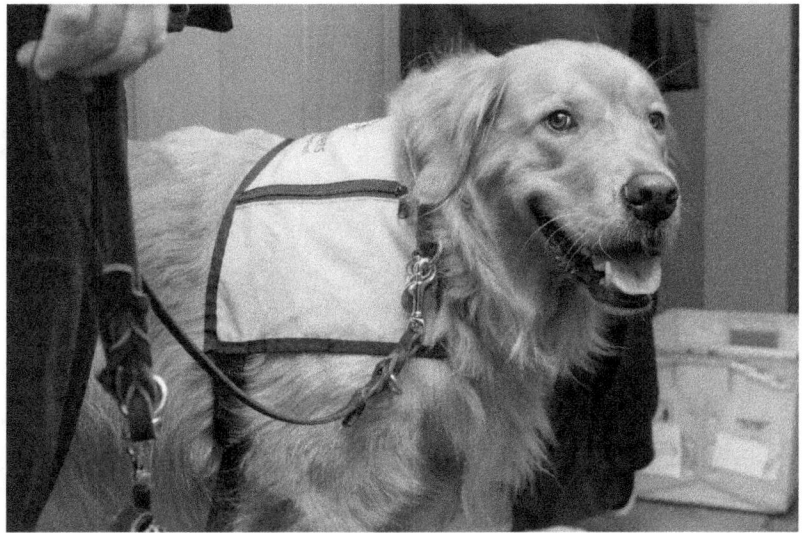

Photo courtesy of Pet Partners

# CHAPTER III
# METHODS AND PROCEDURES

## Introduction

The primary purpose of this empirical phenomenological study was to explore perspectives, attitudes, beliefs, and experiences of registered handler-animal therapy volunteers in New York State on transitioning this intervention from institutional facilities to include community-based environments. The secondary purpose of this empirical phenomenological study was to assess how willing registered handler-animal therapy volunteers were to practice in community-based settings.

In this chapter the researcher described the phenomenological research method for this study and provided the rationale for selecting an empirical phenomenological approach. The researcher also described the following components of the methodology

for this study: description and selection of study

participants, the role as the researcher, and ethical

considerations. In addition, an account of how the

exploratory questionnaire was created, prepared, and

administered was discussed. Lastly, the researcher

discussed the tools for data collection and analysis as

well as threats to data quality.

## Research Design and Rationale

For the purpose of this study, institutional setting

referred to a facility where individuals were given

inpatient status. Inpatient status is characterized as 24-

hour care while living at a specific facility location.

Conversely, community setting referred to an

environment where individuals were considered out-

patient. Out-patient status is flexible and services vary

based on individuals' needs (McCall, 2001). With this

differentiation, the research questions that guided the

focus of this study were the following:

1.      Which attributes of institutional settings (i.e.

        nursing homes, hospitals, rehabilitation facilities)

        assist in the utilization of registered handler-

        animal therapy practices?

2.      What barriers may exist in transitioning registered

        handler-animal therapy practices to community

        settings (i.e. in home services, senior centers,

        adult day care programs)?

3.      How willing are registered handlers to practice in

        community settings?

While researchers have studied the benefits of

animal-assisted therapy on the physical and emotional

state of patients residing in an institutional setting for a

period of time, minimal-to-no research has been

completed on the utilization and adaptation of animal-assisted therapy in community-based settings. The

animal therapy program involved in this study was one of

the leading organizations in New York State and trains

the registered handler and the handler is responsible for

training the animal. In addition, the handler is not

required to be a mental health professional versed in

animal therapy techniques nor is the animal required to

have undergone formal therapy training. As such, the

service provided is registered handler-animal therapy,

which is an adaptation of animal-assisted therapy. To

better understand this notion, a phenomenological study

was implemented.

For Creswell (2009), a qualitative

phenomenological design involves an in-depth inquiry in

order to better understand lived human experiences as

described and reported by study participants. Patton

(2002) elaborated that phenomenological research can

be conducted with a person or a group of people.

Moustakas (1994) asserted the empirical

phenomenological approach involves the provision of a comprehensive description by people who have lived the identified experience. Through reflection and analysis of these descriptions, additional insight and meaning can be revealed within "… the context of a particular situation" (Moustakas, 1994, p. 14), which is the goal of phenomenological research. Because the primary goal of this study was to explore the experiences of registered handler-animal therapy volunteers in institutional settings to assess the prospect of transitioning services to community-based settings, an empirical phenomenological design was most appropriate.

The target sample size range was 15 to 20 individuals who were registered handler-animal therapy volunteers in New York State. Implementing an empirical phenomenological study research study allowed for exploration using open-ended research questions directed towards individuals with firsthand experience

(Creswell, 2009; Patton, 2002). This form of inquiry provided for compelling results as the description of the lived experience is critical in phenomenological research. While the rationale for selecting an empirical phenomenological approach was valid, it was important to consider the role as the researcher.

## Role of the Researcher

In qualitative research the researcher is an instrument of exploration. Through various techniques including observation, interpretation, or evaluation of study findings, a qualitative researcher is an integral component of the study (Creswell, 2009). The researcher's role involved relying on various forms of evidence through what is known as triangulation (Yin, 2009). As such, the researcher was responsible in effectively navigating the agency website for contact information, creating and disbursing the consent forms, maintaining documentation for privacy purposes, and

collecting and extensively analyzing results. The data

collection tool for was an open format questionnaire and

was created based on literature review (Frieson, 2010;

Hudson, 2010; King, 2007) and five follow up telephone

interviews conducted with study participants who agreed

to participate by providing their contact information.

Additional questionnaires and telephone

interviews were unnecessary to satisfy saturation of

data. Saturation of data occurred when the researcher

no longer was able to identify seemingly or obviously

new information. If a point of data saturation was not

met, the researcher would have requested additional

study subjects if the targeted number of responses was

not fulfilled, available responses were too varied, or

repetitive themes or patterns were not evident. Through

collaboration with the research study committee,

saturation or sufficient detail of responses was

determined.

## Methodology

### Participant Selection Logic

Participants in this empirical phenomenological study were at least 18 years of age, either male or female, registered handlers, and volunteered in New York State. Participants were selected using a purposive, homogenous sampling frame. According to Patton (2002), a homogeneous sample involves a group of people with similar experiences or backgrounds, allowing for in depth analysis. In this study, the participants were registered handler-animal therapy volunteers. Because the focus of this study was on registered handler-animal intervention, it was essential individuals recruited to participate underwent training. In the literature review conducted, one organization had been referenced as the leading entity in this field. Since the 1970s, the participating therapy animal program

have screened and trained handlers. Because the

organization trains the handler and not the animal, the

individual is considered to be a registered volunteer

upon completion of the training. As of 2012, there were

over 10,000 trained individuals nationwide providing

handler-animal interventions in hospice centers, nursing

homes, hospitals, and schools.

The prerequisites to become a registered handler

were: individuals had to be at least 10 years of age,

have written permission, and guaranteed

accompaniment to all visits with a parent or guardian.

Handlers who were 18 years of age and older were

unaccompanied, and cats or dogs had to be at least one

year old. For this study, the participants had to be 18

years of age or older and partner with a canine for visits.

There are four stages involved in becoming a registered

handler.

The first stage is required course work to be

completed by the prospective handler. An individual can attend a handler-training course or complete the home study course or participate in the online handler course. If attending a training course, the individual must register in his or her state or a surrounding state. The in person workshop is eight hours in length. If no in-person training courses were available, then completing the online course is the next available option. Individuals purchased the online course and have one year or three attempts to complete the multiple-choice questions. Whether completed in person or online, the individual must have a certificate of completion in order to proceed.

The second stage was to undergo an animal health screening. A qualified veterinarian must examine the animals. Documentation of all required vaccinations and exam results must be provided within the previous six months. Once the handler and the animal screening requirements have been met, prospective handlers can proceed to the third stage, which involves a team evaluation (the individual and animal). Similar to Stage 1, individuals can select their state or surrounding state to register for an evaluation appointment. Team evaluation sessions are 30 minutes in length and require the team to pass all requirements in the skills and aptitude screening. This source exists, but is not provided here to maintain confidentiality. In New York City, there are seven team evaluators. The team has two chanced to attempt to pass and to finalize the registration process.

The fourth and final stage involves submission of paperwork following a successful evaluation. Paperwork is processed within 3 to 4 weeks, after which an acceptance letter, identification badge, and animal tag will arrive. It is recommended the handler have these items available when scheduling or making visits. For liability insurance purposes, each visit is limited to two hours, regardless of location. Each facility has specific qualifications and protocol that registered handler-animal therapy teams must adhere to in order to volunteer at

the site. Volunteers are responsible to seek locations

and/or events where services can be provided. If

registered handler volunteers are interested in becoming

a team evaluator (50 hours) or an instructor (100 hours),

volunteer hours must be documented and the individual

must have been a handler for at least two years. Lastly,

registered handler-animal therapy teams are required to

provide a registration fee and undergo a team evaluation

every two years.

Adhering to the components of a homogeneous

sample, which requires access to a specific sub-group

(Patton, 2002), it was imperative the researcher be able

to contact registered handler-animal therapy teams for

this study. The principal criteria for study participants

included: (a) being a registered handler through the

agency, (b) the registered handler's contact information

was available on the agency website, (c) the registered

handler had access to a computer with Internet access,

and (d) the handler was fluent in the English language.

Names of volunteer teams, instructors, and evaluators

were available for public use through the program's

website, which the researcher searched for volunteers

listed in New York State. A list was generated with each

professional's name, city, state, and e-mail address. To

attain sufficient data and establish saturation of results,

the goal was to obtain 15 to 20 responses to the

exploratory questionnaire created for this study and

conduct five follow up telephone interviews.

## Instrumentation: Preparing the Questionnaire

No validated questionnaires were found in

existing literature exploring the perspectives of

registered handler-animal therapy teams on transitioning

this intervention from the institution to community-based

settings. Following a thorough literature review, a

research questionnaire to explore the experiences,

perspectives, and observations of study participants was

developed. This electronic questionnaire consisted of six

demographic questions: three dichotomous (yes/no)

questions, one nominal scale (gender) question, and two

ordinal scale (age, number of years practiced) questions

for demographic purposes. The 13 open-ended

questions on the questionnaire inquired about the

participants' experiences and observations as registered

handlers and their perspectives on transitioning this

intervention from institutions to community-based

settings. The questionnaire did not provide information

about animal-assisted therapy or its benefits.

The rationale for beginning the questionnaire with

closed ended demographic questions was to ease the

participant into answering prompts in length. Responses

to demographic questions were considered during the

data analysis process to identify gender, age, and/or

years of experience differences. The researcher pre-

coded and coded the data to identify themes and/or

patterns. A similar process was conducted with

responses to the open-ended questions.

The majority of questions were in open format,

allowing participants to provide thoughts and opinions on

a specific prompt, indicative of qualitative research

(Patton, 2002). These open format questions did not

provide predetermined responses; the extent to which a

question was answered was the choice of the

participant. This format of questioning was vital in

soliciting data, because the focus of this study was to

obtain insight from the lived experiences of the

registered handler volunteer regarding the transition of

this intervention from the institution to community-based

settings.

The questions were phrased to avoid bias and

assumptions. In an effort to minimize redundancy and

inaccuracy, the questionnaire was carefully reviewed

and revised by the researcher and peer validated by the

dissertation committee. The researcher created an

account via www.surveymonkey.com and piloted the

questionnaire with the first five respondents. Revisions

and adjustments to the questionnaire were made as

needed in order to complete and finalize the

questionnaire for full distribution by January 2013.

In an effort to maintain the ethical integrity of this

study, the researcher created a letter of cooperation

reviewed and signed for organizational permission. A

call for participation and researcher information was then

provided in an email to registered handlers in New York

State.

The decision to create and distribute an

exploratory questionnaire as the primary data collection

tool rather than solely conducting interviews or a focus

group was based on the following: (a) the geographical

location (i.e. metropolitan and upstate region of New

York) of potential study participants, (b) locating an

accessible meeting area that is equidistant in travel time

for potential study participants, (c) the restricted

technological ability to record and transcribe interviews and dialogue via telephone or Skype, and (d) consideration of potential study participants' personal and professional schedules. As such, the creation and distribution of an exploratory questionnaire via www.surveymonkey.com provided study participants an opportunity to share experiences and insights at their scheduling discretion with minimal hindrances.

In an effort to further expand upon the phenomenological analysis process initiated by the exploratory questionnaire, study participants could opt to participate in a follow-up telephone interview. The researcher's goal was to conduct a minimum of five telephone interviews in addition to the responses to the questionnaire for analysis. The questionnaire (Appendix A) was created and available for completion on the website. Consent forms were created and included in an email as an attached document to inform participants of the purpose of the study at various stages of the process as a component of ethical protection.

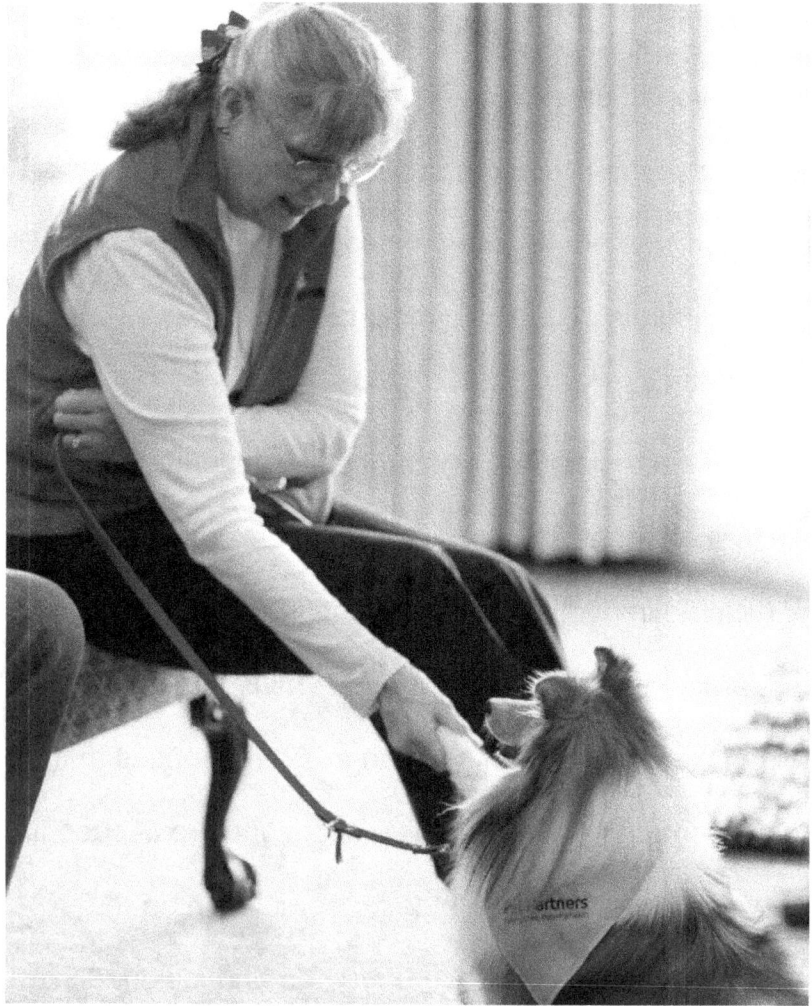

Photo courtesy of Pet Partners

## Ethical Considerations

It was recommended the researcher provide a report of personal and professional information (Patton, 2002). The researcher included personal experience and/or training related to the topic being explored, how the researcher obtained contact information of study participants, and funding sources if applicable. This report was in a cover letter format and distributed via email to study participants prior to the informed consent process.

For Stake (1995), it is the researcher's responsibility to protect study participants from harm by fully informing participants of the purpose of the study as well as obtaining written consent to participate. Prior to completing the questionnaire on the website host, registered handlers were required to electronically sign and return the voluntary consent form to me via email.

The form stated the following: 1) participation is voluntary; 2) the information obtained will be and remain anonymous; 3) the responses made are at the discretion of the participant; and 4) withdrawal from the study can be done so at any time without penalty or consequence. Upon electronic receipt of the consent form, instructions to access the questionnaire were provided in an email to the participant.

The researcher was also ethically accountable to the academic institution supporting this qualitative study. No participants were contacted and no data was collected or analyzed until the researcher received approval of the dissertation proposal from the dissertation committee members. Upon approval, the researcher submitted an application to the Walden University Institutional Review Board (IRB) to receive permission to begin research before contacting study participants, distributing the questionnaire, collecting or analyzing data. IRB approval # is 12-17-12-0167807.

## Data Collection

Data collection occurred in two phases using
www.surveymonkey.com. The first phase involved
creating the questionnaire following the prompts
indicated on the website. A survey link was provided to
the researcher to disperse via email to study
participants. The second phase was managing
responses to the survey. The researcher used the
website host to specify survey restrictions, including a
due date, time expiration for completion, and providing
access to the link one per IP address so participants
were not completing the survey multiple times.
Essentially, the website host was accumulating raw case
data for analysis (Patton, 2002).

The survey was open to participants for six
weeks, in which the researcher collected raw data from
the website host on a weekly basis. The contact

information of study participants who opted to participate in a follow-up telephone interview was tracked in a spreadsheet. The target sample of this study was 15 to 20 responses to the questionnaire and a minimum of five telephone interviews from registered handlers volunteering their services in New York State. If recruitment resulted in too few participants, the researcher would have reengaged recruitment efforts by attending public events hosted by the New York City Coordinator to obtain additional study participants.

Participants who completed the survey received an email upon exiting the study. The email included the following: 1) an expression of gratitude for their time and involvement in completing the survey, 2) notification that a follow up email and/or telephone call (if preferred) may be conducted to confirm preliminary findings, and 3) upon study completion and approval, study findings would be dispersed and used for program purposes. Once data was collected, it was analyzed.

## Data Analysis

The analysis of qualitative multiple case study data involves comparing, interpreting, and identifying patterns (Stake, 1995). For Saldaña (2009), pre-coding is an opportunity to identify key phrases or passages prior to conducting the structured analysis process. In addition, as a first time researcher, it is encouraged that the coding process is a hands on experience to assist in critical thinking and interpretation (Saldaña, 2009). As such, the researcher had a hard copy of each passage on a separate page to highlight and circle key terms, which were referred to as the researcher created potential codes to be used. The researcher utilized the website host and spreadsheets for organizational purposes and processed the analysis by pre-coding the data.

Since the questionnaire included closed- and

open-format questions, the analyses differed.

Responses to open format questions were provided in a

'Summary Report' available through the website host

and was converted to a spreadsheet format. Once the

data was converted, each passage was printed on a

separate spreadsheet for the pre-coding process. The

telephone interviews were transcribed for data

conversion purposes. For phenomenological studies

using survey methods, the coding styles of attribute,

values, and theming the data were appropriate.

Attribute coding can be used for all qualitative

studies particularly for research involving multiple

participants, which is indicative of this study. According

to Saldaña (2009):

… dates, time frames, and routine actions that

participants mention, and the names of people

and programs can be coded as such to reveal

organizational, hierarchal, or chronological flows

from the data, especially if multiple participants

with differing perspectives are involved. (p. 57)

Similarly, values coding can represent

participant's perspectives, values and beliefs. An

exploration of these three constructs is the primary goal

of this study. Lastly, theming the data or the outcome of

the coding and interpretive process is an inclusive

description of results. Themes can also be ideas or

recommendations explicated from participant information

(Saldaña, 2009), which had the potential to delve upon

the secondary goal of this study.

Once the researcher completed the pre-coding

process, the data was typed into a spreadsheet to assist

in viewing 100% of the responses for content analysis to

identify patterns or themes (Patton, 2002). The

researcher conducted an inductive analysis by starting

with a thorough reading of the codes to become familiar

with the content. During this review, it was possible the

researcher would engage in the coding process for a second or third time, further compiling the code list.

The researcher then compared all responses, focusing on content that repeated or restated by other respondents. Through interpretation of concepts or key phrases, the researcher identified patterns and/or themes that emerged from the data (Patton, 2002). Using the spreadsheet and website host, charts, and graphs were created for visual purposes. Analysis of open format questions were more time intensive and reflective compared to the closed format questions.

Responses to closed format questions were relatively easy to code. The website host offered an 'Analyze Results' option, including custom reports to display results specified by the researcher. In this study, Questions 1- 6 were tallied by the website program. The responses were counted and transferred to a spreadsheet. The numbers and/or percentages, otherwise termed as descriptive statistics were used to summarize the study sample. Detailed descriptions of

findings assisted the researcher in maintaining validity

and reliability of results.

## Data Quality and Issues of Trustworthiness

Unlike quantitative methods, validity (external

consistency) and reliability (internal consistency) can be

obtained through repeated experimental measures;

qualitative research requires the researcher to be

consistent and accurate throughout research procedures

(Creswell, 2009). To maintain validity, the researcher

utilized strategies of member checking, rich description,

and clarifying bias.

The objective of member checking is to ensure

accuracy of study information. The initial recruitment of

study participants via the "Find Volunteer Teams,

Instructors, & Evaluators" tab on the website was the

first step of the member checking process. The web

page generated a list of the professionals name, city,

state, and preferred email address to review for general

themes. Following data analysis and compilation of

themes and subthemes, the researcher re-contacted

study participants providing an opportunity for them to

comment on the preliminary findings (Creswell, 2009;

Yin, 2009). The primary method of re-contact was

through email, however, if a participant preferred a

telephone conversation, the researcher scheduled an

appointment. With accurate study findings, the

researcher was also able to provide rich descriptions.

When study findings are presented with rich

descriptions, the themes and perspectives explored

become more realistic and feasible to the reader

(Creswell, 2009). Termed as transferability, study

descriptions and the varied sample involved would be

conveyed substantially. While the element of a physical

environment was absent through the use of a website

host, the creation of graphs or charts were used to

supplement the written analysis. A narrative of present

bias was also provided.

To address bias in qualitative research, it is

recommended the researcher be honest with readers in

terms of how study findings were impacted by the

researcher's personal background (Creswell, 2009). This

narrative provided transparency of study findings as well

as maintained the credibility of the research (Saldaña,

2009). The concern of bias was addressed first by

distribution of a cover letter with information of the

researcher and reiterated in the narrative following the

data analysis process. Throughout the data analysis

procedure, the researcher also practiced reliability

methods.

Reliability in qualitative research or the

consistency of the researcher's approach to the study

involves attention to detail and organization (Creswell,

2009; Yin, 2009). The researcher utilized multiple

sources to organize and understand the data to establish

dependability for triangulation. It was previously

discussed the researcher used the website host to view

completed questionnaires to gain understanding of the

content. During this process, the researcher also

monitored for typos, grammatical errors, or questions

that were left blank. Mistakes were tracked in a

spreadsheet document and discussed in the narrative as

such observations can impact overall data quality and

analysis. All spreadsheet documents for tracking and

coding purposes were reviewed and compared

frequently to ensure the coding process was consistent

for the duration of the study. Lastly, the researcher kept

a reflective journal to monitor interpretations as well as

maintain regular communication with the researcher's

committee to establish 'confirmability,' thus ensuring

best practices of research were utilized.

## Conclusion

This chapter discussed the methodology used to design this empirical, phenomenological study. A rationale for selecting an empirical, phenomenological approach was provided as well as a description of study participants, the researcher's role, and the preparation involved in creating the questionnaire. The researcher also provided discussion on ethical considerations of the study, the data collection and analysis process, and threats to data quality involved in conducting this research. The following chapter will synthesize the findings and results from the study.

# CHAPTER IV
# FINDINGS

## Introduction

The purpose of this phenomenological, qualitative study was to explore the beliefs, experiences, perspectives, and observations of registered handler-animal therapy individuals who volunteered their services in New York State in relation to community-based animal-assisted therapy. Registered handlers from an organization referenced in the literature review as the primary animal therapy program throughout the Unities States were selected. Registered handlers responded to closed ended questions for demographic purposes and open-ended questions created to explore and better understand reasons for utilizing this service primarily in institutional settings, potential barriers in

transitioning to community-based settings, and the

prospective willingness of handlers to volunteer their

services in community locations. These concepts are

stated in detail as the research questions for this study:

1.    Which attributes of institutional settings (i.e.

      nursing homes, hospitals, rehabilitation facilities)

      assist in the utilization of registered handler-

      animal therapy practices?

2.    What barriers may exist in transitioning registered

      handler-animal therapy practices to community

      settings (i.e. in home services, senior centers,

      adult day care programs)?

3.    How willing are registered handlers to practice in

      community settings?

In this chapter, the researcher discussed the pilot

study and final launch of the research study,

demographics of study participants, data collection and

analysis procedures, evidence of trust-worthiness, and

results of this research study.

## Pilot Study

To obtain participants for the pilot study, the

researcher distributed a call for participation email to

registered handlers in New York City. Approximately 250

names were listed on the publicly accessible website,

with approximately 50 emails generated message errors

or were no longer active (i.e. email bounce back). Of the

200 active emails, the first five responses to the call for

participation were selected for the pilot study of this

research project. Consent forms were distributed via

email and the five pilot study participants returned the

forms to the researcher's email with electronic

signatures. Upon receipt of the consent form, the

researcher provided each pilot study participant the link

to the electronic version of the www.surveymonkey.com

questionnaire as well as the questionnaire in a word

processing software format. Pilot study participants were

requested to complete the electronic version of the

questionnaire and provide feedback on the ease of use,

grammar, and level of comprehension using a track

changes feature in the word processor software

document. The duration of the pilot study was 2-3

weeks.

Pilot study participants reported no concerns

related to the www.surveymonkey.com link; however,

participants reported revisions to certain phrases were

needed. Questions 8, 9, 13, 15, 18, 19, and 20 used the

phrase *handler-animal interventions*. Pilot study

participants reported the term *handler-animal*

*interactions* was appropriate. Questions 19 and 20 used

the phrase *profession*. Pilot study participants reported

that the term *service* was appropriate. Question 12 used

the phrase *limitations* associated with using a canine in

therapy. Pilot study participants reported the term

*concerns* was appropriate. Lastly, Question 14 (How

would you describe the benefits of and/or limitations

associated with the facility/institution in which handler-

animal services are provided?) was removed as pilot

study participants reported this question was "redundant"

and "not necessary" because remaining questions

addressed this content.

The researcher revised the questionnaire based

on the pilot study participants responses and created a

new www.surveymonkey.com link for the newer

electronic version. The questionnaire was distributed to

final launch study participants included six closed ended

questions for demographic purposes and 13 open-ended

questions, totaling 19 questions.


## Final Launch of Research Study


To obtain participants for the final launch of this

research study, the researcher redistributed the call for

participation email to registered handlers in New York

City. The call for participation email was also distributed

to registered handlers in Queens, Bronx, Staten Island,

Brooklyn (considered to be New York City), Nassau,

Suffolk, Westchester, Rockland, Orange, Putnam,

Ulster, and Dutchess counties to include areas

considered to be New York State. From these areas,

approximately 439 names were listed on the publicly

accessible website, with approximately 100 emails

bouncing back with error messages or were no longer

active (i.e. email bounce back). Of the 339 active emails,

the researcher received approximately 12 email

responses and/or telephone calls inquiring for additional

information – these individuals decided not to pursue

participation. However, 28 individuals responded to the

call for participation and a consent form was distributed

via email. Of the 28 individuals, 21 consent forms were

returned to the researcher's email with an electronic

signature. Upon receipt of the consent form, the

researcher provided each study participant the

www.surveymonkey.com link to the electronic

questionnaire. The duration of the call for participation

process and availability of the electronic questionnaire

was six weeks. Of the 21 individuals who returned a

consent form, 18 provided responses to the electronic

questionnaire.

## Demographics

The composition of the 18 respondents included

three men (16.67%) and 15 women (83.33%). One

individual reported being between 36 and 40 years old

(5.56%) while the remaining 17 reported being older

than 41 years old (94.44%). All respondents (100%)

reported being a registered handler.

Photo courtesy of Pet Partners

Of the 18 respondents, five individuals (27.78%)

reported being a registered handler for less than a year,

five individuals (27.78%) reported being a registered

handler for 1-3 years, four individuals (22.22%) reported

being a registered handler for 4-6 years, three

individuals (16.67%) reported being a registered handler

for 7-10 years, and one individual reported being a

registered handler for 11 to 15 years as illustrated in

Figure 1.

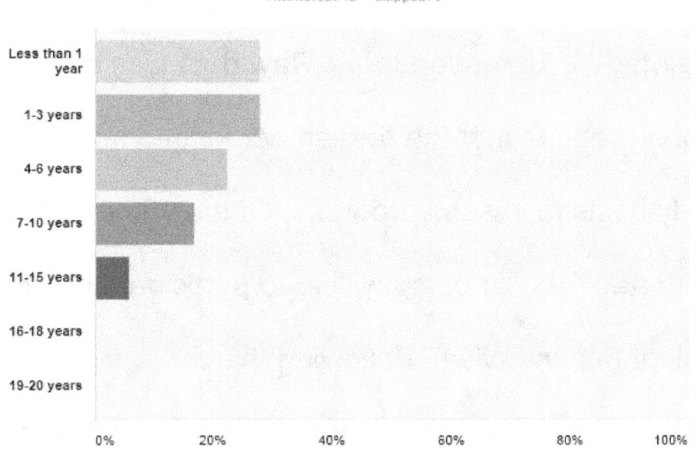

Figure 1 - Illustration of Length of Time as Registered Handler (in years)

Of the 18 respondents, 16 individuals (94.12%)

reported they used a canine as the primary therapy

animal, one individual (5.88%) reported they did not, and

one individual skipped this question.

## Data Collection

Questions 1-5 and 13-15 were completed by 18

respondents. Questions 6-12, 16, 18, and 19 were

completed by 17 respondents. Question 17 was

completed by 16 respondents. Raw data was stored in

the host website that the researcher logged into on a

weekly basis to assess progress. Of the 18 respondents,

all reported (100%) being willing to participate in a follow

up telephone interview. Following the conclusion of the

six weeks for participants to complete the electronic

questionnaire, all raw data was converted and exported

as a spreadsheet as well as a portable document file

(pdf) to be used for data analysis purposes.

In addition, five individuals were selected at

random to participate in a follow up telephone interview.

The researcher contacted potential interview participants

via email requesting an attached consent form be

returned and to respond with a preferred contact

number, as well as preferred days and times to complete

the interview. Upon receipt of the consent form with an

electronic signature, the researcher scheduled the five

follow up telephone interviews. The duration of

scheduling and conducting of interviews was

approximately two weeks. Each telephone interview was

conducted in the researcher's home office and was

audio-recorded using a sound recorder. Each interview

was saved as an audio (wma) file and referenced for

transcription purposes. The researcher projected tat

each interview would be approximately 45 minutes in

length; however, the average interview was 25 to 30

minutes.

An unanticipated difficulty associated with the

data collection process experienced. Not all study

participants were computer or technology savvy.

Participants were able to correspond with the researcher

by email or telephone, but when asked to return the

consent form as an attached document a small number

of the study participants experienced difficulty. However,

alternative approaches were utilized (mailed or faxed

consent form) to proceed with study procedures. Overall,

the data collection process was successful.

## Data Analysis

Coding the responses to closed ended questions

was relatively easy. The website host tracked Questions

1-6 and descriptive statistics (numbers / percentages) of

participants were automatically generated. Responses

were converted and exported to a spreadsheet as well

as a portable document file (pdf) for reporting purposes.

Analysis of open-ended questions began with a

pre-coding process. According to Saldaña (2009), pre-coding is recommended for first time researchers to assist in identifying key phrases or passages prior to conducting the structured analysis process. The researcher printed each open-ended question and associated responses on a separate page. Using a yellow highlighter, the researcher identified key terms or words that reappeared throughout the responses. These key terms were then transferred to a spreadsheet for organizational purposes.

Using the spreadsheet, the researcher continued with the coding process, identifying appropriate attribute, values, and identifying themes of the data codes. For Saldaña (2009), attribute coding can reveal routine actions or organizational viewpoints useful in that study participants provided anecdotes and experiences related to providing handler-animal therapy services in a variety of settings/environments. Values coding represented participants' beliefs and perspectives while theming the data involved a description of results (Saldaña, 2009).

Because participants were prompted to provide as little

or as much detail in response to each of the 13 open-

ended questions, there were opportunities for

interpretation of content. With this process, the codes of

visit/interaction, acceptance, and exposure/education

were identified (Appendix C).

*Question 8*: How is the canine utilized in handler-

animal interactions?

Respondent 2 stated, "… canine is used for

temporary companionship tactile interaction and to foster

a feeling of warmth and attention and validation. The

canine feels important and useful and the client feels

involved and tended to."

*Question 11*: In your opinion, what are the

benefits, if any, of using a canine as a therapy animal?

Explain.

Respondent 4 stated, "absolute acceptance by

the animal of any adult or child. [The animal is] calm,

sweet natured, reduces blood pressure, and eases

anxiety in all."

*Question 17*: In your opinion, what aspects of

community level handler-animal interactions would help

expand this service? Explain.

Respondent 1 stated, "exposure to the success of

the programs by demonstration of the benefits and

results of the programs."

As previously stated, not all the 18 respondents

completed each prompt of the questionnaire and the

demographics of study participants (gender / age) were

considered as discrepant cases for analysis as

responses had the potential to be skewed. Another

unanticipated discrepancy was the varied writing abilities

of study participants. Some responses were written as

incomplete sentences with mechanical errors (i.e.

spelling, subject verb agreement). While errors made the

researcher more active in the coding process, the

researcher was also responsible in interpreting the

responses to the best of their ability. Nonetheless, the

quality of descriptive data was suitable for coding

purposes.

Photo courtesy of author

## Evidence of Trustworthiness

In Chapter 3, the researcher discussed the need

for member checking, rich description, and clarifying bias

in order to maintain the validity of this research study.

For Creswell (2009), the consistency and accuracy of

research procedures conducted by the researcher are

important in producing credible, transferable,

dependable, and confirmable qualitative data.

Member checking maintains accurate study

information. Following the data analysis and coding

process, the researcher re-contacted study participants

via email. The researcher expressed gratitude for their

time and participation in the research study. The

researcher also provided preliminary findings based on

the identified codes and encouraged feedback (Creswell,

2009; Yin, 2009). The comments received by study

participants were positive and the researcher was

encouraged to complete the research study in a timely

manner so results could be formally distributed. With an

accuracy of study findings, the researcher was able to

proceed to obtain rich descriptions. For Creswell (2009),

rich descriptions or transferability can provide realism and feasibility to study findings. In this way, graphs or charts were created to supplement the written analysis. Rich descriptions also assisted in clarifying bias.

For Creswell (2009), clarifying bias involves the researcher being honest with readers and participants in regards to the potential impact of study findings. Termed as a narrative, the credibility and transparency of study findings will be maintained (Saldaña, 2009). The concern of bias was first addressed with the distribution of the call for participation in the form of a cover letter. The call for participation included information about the researcher and encouraged correspondence to take place. Clarifying bias was also addressed when the five follow up telephone interviews were conducted. While an interview script (Appendix B) was used, slight delineations from the script occurred due to dialogue, questions, and flow of conversation with participants. With a number of data collection and analyses present, the researcher also strived to maintain reliability.

Triangulation, the use of multiple sources to organize and interpret data to establish dependability, was needed (Creswell, 2009; Yin, 2009). The website host was used to store raw data. On a weekly basis for the six week period, the researcher logged into the website to view participant progress. During this time the researcher monitored for typos, grammatical errors, or questions left blank, which were tracked in a spreadsheet document for future discussions on study findings (Appendix H). All spreadsheet documents for tracking and coding purposes were reviewed and compared on a biweekly basis to ensure the coding process was consistent for the duration of the study. Lastly, the researcher maintained a reflective journal in the form of free writing notes to assist the researcher with interpretations of responses. The use of multiple record keeping practices also assisted the researcher in maintaining frequent correspondence with the dissertation committee to establish 'confirmability,' all of which were to ensure best practices of research were utilized.

## Results

As previously stated, this phenomenological, qualitative study was guided by three exploratory research questions. This section addressed each research question and presented supporting data in the form of quotes from questionnaire, interview transcripts, and charts.

### Research Question 1

Which attributes of institutional settings (i.e. nursing homes, hospitals, rehabilitation facilities) assist in the utilization of registered handler-animal therapy practices?

Of the 18 respondents, 17 individuals reported

that they use a canine as the primary therapy animal

(94.12%), one individual does not use a canine (5.88%)

and one individual did not report. The breeds of canines

used for therapy sessions include Whippet, Golden

Retriever (2), Pomeranian, Black Labrador (2), Bouvier

des Flandres, Keeshond, Mixed Breed (3), Standard

Poodle, Brussels Griffon, Greyhound, West Highland

Terrier, Papillon, and Shih Tzu.

**Question #8:** How is the canine utilized in

handler-animal interactions?

Respondent #3 stated:

Qualification are routinely predictable interactions,

low activity, low distractions, must be carried.

Being a part of a handler-animal team allows me

to communicate with the residents about their

experience with animals in the past. I allow the

residents or students to pet Satchmo, give him treats and sit on their laps. We also try to entertain with a few tricks.

Respondent #13 stated: "After asking if a person would like to visit the dog, I command the dog to 'visit' and he stands by the person to be petted and spoken to. He often rests his head in their lap."

Respondent #14 stated: "She visits ill people in a hospital. She interacts with challenged children. She is read to by an autistic child."

**Question #9:** In what types of facilities/institutions have you practiced handler animal interactions with a canine (nursing homes, hospitals, hospices)?

Respondent #2 stated: "Assisted living facility, nursing home, and public children's library."

Respondent #13 stated: "Nursing homes, assisted living facilities, day care facility for people with traumatic brain injuries, day care facility for adults recovering from substance abuse."

Respondent #15 stated: "Pediatric unit in hospital specializing in orthopedic surgery."

Respondent #16 stated: "Hospitals, hospice, Ronald McDonald House."


**Question #10:** In these facilities and institutions, what populations have you worked with (children, adults, elderly) diagnosis of chronic mental or health condition?

Respondent #2 stated: "Able bodied children and senior citizens with some physical or cognitive disability."

Respondent #13 stated: "Mainly adults, some elderly, with various health issues: dementia, blindness, inability to walk and/or talk, limited communication ability."

Respondent #15 stated:

Children with orthopedic problems stemming from accidents, birth defect, and cerebral palsy. Some of the children are from other countries and don't speak English. Unless there are some cultural

issues around animals as pets, most of the

children respond favorably to the dog.

Respondent #16 stated: "Babies, children, adults,

staff (you would be surprised the affect therapy pups

have on the staff just by watching), elderly, terminally ill,

children with learning disabilities."


**Question #11:** In your opinion, what are the

benefits, if any, of using a canine as a therapy animal?

Explain.

Respondent #7 stated:

It is well documented the mere presence of a dog

can lower blood pressure and put a client or

patient at ease. Time and time again I have

observed how people will relax and often open up

when interacting with our dogs. They smile,

become animated, start talking, etc. This is

especially true at the Behavior Health Center we

visit as a major hospital. We do not know the

history of the patients we visit with, but on several

occasions we have witnessed small breakthroughs

because of their interaction with our dogs.

Photo courtesy of author

Respondent #14 stated:

In the hospital, a dog is soothing to the touch, they are comforting to people who are scared or alone. The dogs bring a smile to sad faces. For challenged children, they make them feel special and allow them to learn about dogs and their care. They learn to touch, brush, and even walk or talk. That makes them very proud, and makes them feel important.

Respondent #10 stated:

Almost too many to list; in a hospital the dog not only helps the patients but the visitors and the hospital staff; my dog once sat with someone waiting in ambulatory surgery – her presence was immeasurable; another time my dog encouraged a patient during physical therapy to walk further than she ever had before; another time a child visiting a parent in hospice care got to play with my dog for a while … invaluable.

**Interview Question #3:** Based on your

experiences as a registered handler-animal therapy

team, how would you describe the purpose of this

service? Please specify the locations in which you

volunteer as well.

The purpose is, I feel genuinely, is to bring some

positive feelings to whomever we are visiting. It

could be a break in their day; it could be some

increased conversation, with the others. I don't

know what politically correct word that you want to

use, some say consumer some people say

patient, but anyway to the visitees to just bring

them some positive emotion. I have worked in

senior facilities, you know some people with

dementia. I have been doing this a long time. This

is my second job that I do it with. I've done this in

a children's rehab hospital and to libraries. I am

also a humane educator, so I go into a lot of preschools. I do prevention and kindness to animals.

I have gone into adult group homes. I haven't

done hospitals specifically. I guess this is where

my particular boundaries blur ... as a therapist, I

use my dogs in sessions with children. Many of

whom are on the autistic spectrum. (Interviewee

3)

## Research Question 2

What barriers may exist in transitioning registered

handler-animal therapy practices to community settings

(i.e. in home services, senior centers, adult day care

programs)?

**Question #12:** In your opinion, what are the

concerns, if any, of using a canine as a therapy animal?

Explain.

Respondent #7 stated:

Concerns center around stress levels for the dog.
A handler must always be aware of what their dog
can and cannot tolerate and to be watchful for
signs of stress in the animal. Handlers must know
when or if the dog needs a break and how to
manage the animal is those signs of stress are
present. Another concern would be an
unpredictable patient that could in any way, harm
the animal. In most facilities a client or patient
would not be brought into the room or be on a list
to visit with a dog if they did not wish to do so.
However, it is possible that this situation could
arise and the handler must know how to manage
the situation should it arise for the best interest of
the patient as well as the animal. It is very
important that the dog not become so stressed
out that they shut down and reach the point of
relating the visits to a negative experience.

Respondent #16 stated:

The right training, the ability to monitor a dog and handlers progress and offer support and feedback. For instance, some does lose interest in therapy (can be due to many factors) or some handlers lose interest or force their dogs to do things/tricks they do not want. Also, the animals and handlers need environments where they are truly welcomed and appreciated. Having the support of the staff/family allows the therapy to be all it can be.

Respondent #17: "It is tough and stressful on the dog. People are sometimes too rough on the dog and startle the dog. The handler must always be alert and put the best interests of the dog first."

**Question #15:** What would be the difficulties involved in providing handler-animal services in community settings? Explain.

Respondent #2 stated:

It has proven very difficult for us to get a therapy

dog into someone's personal residence, due to

the uniqueness of the layout each time of the

home and the unpredictable nature of the home

owner. In inpatient, there is always a facility

representative there to assist. Senior citizen

centers may have more revolving population

whereas inpatient the population is consistent.

Respondent #4 stated:

In home settings may be challenging, as it would

require more animal-handlers, as it is a one-on-

one situation. Whereas, in a senior day-care

facility, for example, you may only need a few

animal-handlers in a large group. Animal-handler

safety could be a concern in a home setting as it

would be a less controlled environment.

Respondent 16 stated:

Getting animal teams to the homebound would be

a transportation issue. Setting up a regular

schedule of visits at senior centers would involve

another responsibility for the managers and

directors of the centers. The centers would have

to be willing to add the service.

Respondent #17 stated: "The environment would

have to be controlled for the dog's safety and well-being.

The handler would have to know that the community

setting was stable and consistent."


**Question #16:** What modifications to handler-

animal interactions do you recommend for community

level services? Explain.

Respondent #2 stated:

Start with senior citizen centers and adult day

facilities first, as opposed to in home visits. Get

the staff involved and onboard and vary the days

you visit so guests know when the therapy animal

is coming and they can avoid that room that day if

desired. Educate the clients, without the dogs, as

to the benefit of therapy animals.

Photo courtesy of author

Respondent #9 stated: "You might have to tailor

the teams to the service being provided. Not all teams

are suited for all visits. You would need someone to

match the teams to the sites."

Respondent #10 stated: "Close supervision is

always the most important and the handler being aware

of their animal's signs for stress."

Respondent #13 stated: "Keep groups small so that the animal has an opportunity to interact with each individual.

**Interview Question #5:** With interests in community-based work, I wonder if these services would be appropriate at that level. Before moving forward, can you define of both of these terms (*institutions* and *community*)?

An institutional setting, to me, is a facility that has specific mission to provide, specifically defined form of care. So an institution would be something like a hospital or a school or a facility for those people with emotional issues whether its adults or children. A prison can be an institution. They are kind of self-governing bodies with a mission. A nursing home would be an institution like a hospital. A community-based facility is something that would be like an adult day care center or library or senior center that is housed in a part of a religious institution or that has a building of their own somehow. Sometimes funded by the state or charity. It doesn't have state rules or regulations that they have to function and live like a hospital would or rehab center. They do have missions and goals. But the regulations are somewhat different. Sometimes a school would be a nice if the 'read to the dog' programs, let's say in public schools, rather in just private schools in the library. Community is where you are everyday, where you live. An institution, I think in the minds of a lot of people, are where they service and care is provided when there is a crisis in your life, whether it is health or emotional. (Interviewee 4)

**Interview Question #8.** If you were selected as the "model" registered handler and were asked to share with others your three biggest secrets on how to modify the program structure in order to serve more older adults in community-based settings, what would they be and why?

Oh, wow. That is a heavy question. Wow. I would try to build confidence within the program and to build it that it's not fluff. Oh we are having puppies today. It's like I would want to push people to understand that it really does make a difference in your day. That it is just not, oh should I play checkers or meet with the puppies? I think that even though they may not speak or they may not be able to understand what you are possibly saying. The fact that they are there made such a difference. I would push the program, meaning I would make it concrete not just we may have the dogs here this week, we may not. I think when they realize it is something everybody is taking

seriously, that it is concrete that it is something

they will have to look forward to it and they can

really build upon it. The first experience with an

animal may not be the best. They may be a little

nervous, the dog may be a little bit uncomfortable.

It could be for very several reasons. It could be

the environment is too warm, the climate is not

suitable, so on and so forth or the staff wasn't

trained. So that's something else. The staff would

be on board completely to ensure that the

environment is amendable to pet therapy. For

example in pediatrics, we have shortened our

stays because pediatrics tends to be very, very

warm. I have Shihtzus and they are usually in full

coat and glory. They just can't handle a room that

is 80 degrees. It is just too warm. So it's a shame,

but you know and I understand it's a hospital

environment, sometimes even when you work

with seniors you they're cold. I did hospice with one particular woman, She was such a doll. She realized that Peebles was always getting overheated. Sometimes we would step out for fresh air and come back in. So what she used to do in the summer, is that she used to have her nurse put on the air conditioning before Peebles got there just to cool off the apartment a little bit, even though she had to put on a sweater. Just so that she could have Peebles there longer cause it made such a difference to her. I think that when they realize that we are there to provide care, comfort, and concern and so on so forth. They have to realize when it's 85 degrees in their room or there is no water or they don't let water bowls on the floor even if it's off in a safe corner so on and so forth, we would have to leave and then no one gets to experience what they could.

(Interviewee 1)

Well, the first one is not really a secret. The secret

is that the dog is the star, not you and don't you

ever forget that. I think too many, unfortunately

too many handlers think that they are the

important to the situation, but it really is the

animal. The second one is that not every situation

might be right for you. The third one is to

remember that you are an ambassador, to smile

and be part of the process. (Interviewee 5)


**Question #18:** In your opinion, what aspects of

community level handler-animal interactions would limit

this service? Explain.

Respondent # 3 stated: "A poorly lit environment,

heavy traffic of people not involved in activity, no

representatives to speak to if something comes up."

Respondent #10 stated: "Often scheduling is an

issue and location of facility. Personally, I can only visit

at certain times because of my work, so having specific

times established by a facility was limiting to me."

Respondent #14 stated: "The only limits I have encountered are distances. There are many places that would be great to visit, but without a car they are usually out of reach."

Respondent #17 stated: "The community would need to assign an employee/volunteer to make sure the animal has a consistent and safe environment for each and every visit."

**Interview Question #2:** In qualitative interviewing, asking a hypothetical question is an excellent approach to exploring how you would handle a situation or what your hopes for a situation would be. Therefore, if you could change just one thing about your current practices in terms of how a canine is used in registered-handler interventions, what would it be?

Oh wow, if I could change one thing, I think if the staff was better prepared for the intervention, so to speak. Some staff are not animal friendly. I can

understand that and I can appreciate that, but I'm

not coming in to gain attention for myself or the

animal. We are actually coming into work and we

are coming into aid in the healing process or if we

are in the library an education process, so on and

so forth. Sometimes the staff makes faces. Or

let's say they don't like dogs or have had bad

experiences with pets in the past or other

people's pets and their negative reactions, even

though it is automatic for them, it's who they are.

It doesn't help the therapy in anyway.

(Interviewee 1)


**Interview Question #6:** The transition of

providing registered handler-animal therapy services

from institutions to communities could be difficult in

terms of establishing community partnerships and a

client population. How does that make you feel?

I would really hope that the community would

could come together and see a video or they could

be exposed to the benefits of registered handlers

and their teams and the dogs or the donkeys. I just

read an article that there is a llama out there that

is a pet partner. That animals have a special touch

with people that are receptive to it. If anything it

just makes everybody calm. I've literally seen the

theory where they say the blood pressure just

drops and it does. Somehow animals who are well

natured and have good habits have the ability to

break down fences and break down barriers where

there could be a lot of tension in the room whether

it be cultural or family oriented or so on and so

forth. You bring in a puppy and everyone just goes

… ahh. You melt the room. If you bring in a cat

that is cuddly it just changes the aura and the so-

called feelings in the room. I would hope that the

people who are looking to bring in such a team

into community-based environment would really

give it their all. Just because there are so many

people who are receptive to it once they know the

benefit they know they can achieve. (Interviewee

1)

… how do you get people [handlers]? A lot of

times it is older people who will do it because they

have the time you know, but I'm sixty. I started

when I was 53 or 54 … it's hard for younger adults

to get involved because they have children and

that whole thing … I think that is one of the

reasons, have the energy to do it, but they don't

have the time or they may have the time and not

the energy. (Interviewee 2)

**Interview Question #7:** As you may know,

registered handlers have different approaches when

working with client populations, older adults in particular.

What are your registered handler practices like when

working with older adults?

In my experience, the humans have to be very savvy and very aware of all kinds of things. You need to be really aware of if they are in a wheelchair, are the brakes locked? If their legs are covered by a blanket. You have to be very mindful if the dog wants to get up on the chair next to them. You just have to I think a.) ask the staff and b.) try read the client as best as possible because they are unpredictable at times. They might be sort of sedentary and have a sort of look in their eye and all of a sudden something might trigger them. So you just have to be very mindful of the situation. My own particular problem and I think it is because I am a social worker, is I have to remember not to talk too much and that it is not my visit and let the dog do his work. (Interviewee 3)

Photo courtesy of author

You want me to think of older adults. I think that

you have to have the handler has be aware of

what the older adult is allowed. There has to be

an education process for the handler. Then, we'll

my dog I don't know, but I think all the dogs need

to have experience with the apparatuses and the wheelchairs that kind of stuff. (Interviewee 5)

**Interview Question #9:** If additional registered handler-animal services were provided to additional community environments, particularly for older adults, how could this benefit and/or hinder this volunteer based program?

If you have too many handlers and animals in the room at the same time it distracts. The dogs get distracted and they are not focused on what they are there to do. So doing, sometimes they want to get in as many handlers and animals as they can, they think it's going to be great ... I guess the right time of day is important because some seniors are great until a certain time and then boom, the energy level drops. (Interviewee 2)

## Research Question 3

How willing are registered handlers to practice in community settings?

**Question #13:** How would you describe the purpose of handler-animal interactions?

Respondent #1 stated: "The canines react to the trust and confidence they gain in their relationship while working with the handler."

Respondent #3 stated: "The purpose of the handler-animal interactions is to provide a sense of trust and love."

Respondent # 17 stated: "Create a stress free environment with an individual and animal who only wants the best for the participant. A stress free environment filled with love, laughs, cuteness, cuddles to facilitate healing, learning, and relaxation."

**Question #14:** Do you think that providing

handler-animal services at the community level would be

beneficial (i.e. in home programs, senior centers, adult

day programs)? Explain.

Respondent #3 stated: "Providing handler-animal

services at the community level are more than beneficial;

it provides unconditional love to those who are lonely.

Many no longer have pets to care for and most times, do

not have others that come to visit them."

Respondent #5 stated: "Yes, it's always helpful to

have a positive interaction with dogs or people, it builds

confidence for the individual."

Respondent #16 stated:

Yes, I think it would. Many seniors live alone and

would probably enjoy a visit from a handler-

animal team. I know that in addition to providing

food to the homebound, Meals on Wheels is a

way to check in on someone living alone. A visit

to the senior center would be a change in routine

and provide a chance for people to benefit from

the presence of a sweet animal.

**Question #17:** In your opinion, what aspects of

community level handler-animal interactions would help

expand this service?

Respondent #2 stated: "Community outreach and

education to eliminate any myths or handle

exaggerations. Promote pet therapy at street fairs and

community gatherings. Be consistent with your visits so

the client knows what to expect."

Respondent # 4 stated:

More media and informational exposure of the

benefits of handler-animal interactions to the

general public so they can advocate as well as

community facility executives and boards to

realize the benefits. Whenever I speak to anyone

about animal-assisted therapy, everyone thinks it

is a great idea. Being an ambassador is, of

course, essential, but not enough people really know about it. This is a volunteer effort and more emphasis must be put on recruitment and retention of handlers. Also, funding would be helpful. It becomes the responsibility of the handler to pay for the eight-week training and there may be people who would love to volunteer but do not have the resources to pay.

Respondent # 8 stated: "The more interactions out there, the more exposure gained and more people know about the services, more people would want the services."

Respondent #14 stated: I think it more service providers and individuals better understood the benefits of handler-animal interactions, there would be more demand for such services in the community. In some cases, people aren't even aware of the existence of animal therapy teams.

**Interview Question #9:** If additional registered handler-animal services were provided to additional community environments, particularly for older adults, how could this benefit and/or hinder this volunteer based program?

It would depend on what the program is and what the program's goal is. If the program's goal is to ... have seniors interact, to build positive feelings, and to possibly even have them get up and out of chairs. Sometimes, when I was with certain people, you know it gets depressing being in a hospital after so long you just want to give up or you just not want to get out of bed anymore. So, sometimes I would offer the senior or the patient to lets go for a walk. You know so that Pebbles or Bam-Bam go for a walk. You know if you are up for it lets go for a walk, were I would be happy to take a stroll around the floor with you. It got them out of bed, but sometimes you don't realize what you've been missing until you actually leave your

room. It would depend on, I'm sure, on what the

goal of the program would be, but if the programs

goals were to incorporate some of the ideals of

the pet partner program, to offer fellowship of

nature and comfort of some nature, a laugh or

you know something to boost the mood. Then by

all means incorporate a registered team in that

environment. (Interviewee 1)

I don't see it hindering it at all unless there is not

enough supervision or control of particular visits

and there are incidents. So, I don't see that

happening. I can't think of anything really. I think

the benefit gives, like to see a weekly or monthly

visit so that there is continuity so the older adults

have something to look forward to. It's a great, I

know I am preaching to the choir here, the dogs

are great ice breakers. They really promote

conversation and socialization and I think also

there are ways to perhaps carry over some other

activities. For example if there is arts and crafts,

take pictures of the dogs, make frames for them,

write stories, you know just to totally incorporate

the dog into the community-based life.

(Interviewee 3)

As more and more institutions and community

centers become aware of AAT and what AAT's

can bring to the table in terms of enhancing care

and community life and teaching. I think it might

be a good post professional career. I mean if I

were maybe paid to do this every day, I would,

this is something I would do at this point in my life.

Also, I know that there are schools with students

with learning challenges. I know that reading

assisted education dogs would, I have read about

it, how effective they can be. I think that having

read dogs in that type of school would be a good

thing, not just once a week. As part of the

teaching experience and the learning experience.

(Interviewee 4)

**Question #19:** How willing would you be to

practice in community settings? Explain.

Of the 18 respondents, one individual skipped this

question. The remaining 17 responses are illustrated in

Figure 2:

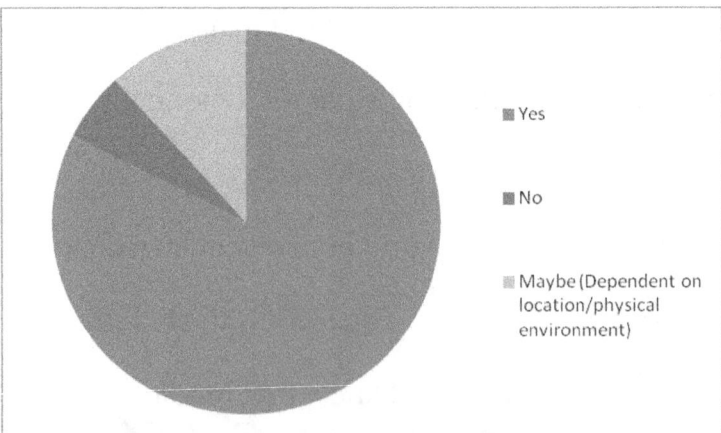

*Figure 2 - Illustration of Handler's Prospective Willingness to*

*Practice in Community Setting.*

Respondent #5 stated: "I am willing and feel I already have practices. I've been to Rotary Club meetings, school fairs, and even had my canine companion at community parades."

Respondent #6 stated: "I would be happy to do this once a week."

Respondent # 9 stated: "Very willing – for the right setting."

**Interview Question #10:** Do you have an experience that you can share with me discussing how willing you may be to volunteer your services as a registered handler-animal therapy team in more community environments?

Oh, a 100%. We already do through hospice and hospice doesn't have to mean that they are on a ventilator and you know it could mean that they have less than a certain amount to live, but they want to live it as fully as they can. Community-

based centers sounds even more exciting

because who doesn't love to throw around a ball

with a dog or watch a dog do tricks. It just boosts

the whole environment of you know, the place.

Yeah it would be totally, you know, what I realized

is that in the beginning when I became a handler,

I thought that I had to kind of specialize. Oh my

dogs are very good with kids, yeah its true they

always were and that's what I thought that is what

they are geared to, but they love everybody. You

know, they don't segregate and that is what they

taught me, to be more open minded as well. Not

only seniors, but seniors of different cultures.

Some cultures believe it or not, especially in

senior centers, some cultures are not fond of

dogs. Some cultures see dogs or other animals

as dirty or that they shouldn't be indoors. I would

love to show them that it really depends on how

the animal is raised and if the animal is

domesticated and they have a kind nature, you

can draw so much comfort from them. Someone

needs laughter, they do have love to give in their

own way and I would love to share it with them.

Yeah, absolutely. (Interviewee 1)

## Conclusion

The research methodology used to collect data on

the beliefs, experiences, perspectives, and observations

of registered handler-animal therapy individuals who

volunteer their services in New York State in relation to

community-based animal-assisted therapy was effective

and produced a significant amount of information on the

topic being explored. It also showed similarities among

participants who completed the exploratory

questionnaire and the individuals who were selected at

random who completed a follow-up telephone interview.

The chapter also provided an overview of the pilot

study and final launch of the research study,

demographics of study participants, data collection and

analysis procedures, evidence of trustworthiness, results

of this research study, and an overview of the limitations

of the study. The researcher derived several themes by

a careful review of data, and comparison to themes

that emerged in the literature review. These were

identified through pre-coding and coding processes. The

themes noted include *visit/interaction* for Research

Question 1, (Chandler, Portrie-Bethke, Barrio Minton,

Fernando, & O'Callaghan, 2010; Wesley, Minatreat and

Watson, 2009), *acceptance* for Research Question 2,

(Cuijpers, Steunenberg, & Van Straten, 2007; King,

2007; Van der Weele, Gussekloo, De Waal, De Craen, &

Van der Mast, 2008) and *exposure /education* for

Research Question 3 (Risley-Curtiss, 2010; , Holley, &

Wolf, 2006; Netting, Wilson, & New, 1987). The

responses provided by participants confirmed, as well as

extended, the knowledge base surrounding each of the

research questions that guided this study. In the

upcoming chapter, an analysis of research findings and

themes are detailed.

# CHAPTER V
# SUMMARY, CONCLUSIONS, AND
# RECOMMENDATIONS

## Introduction

In this chapter, the researcher provides a discussion of the research findings outlined in chapter 4. Through a literature review (Chandler, Portrie-Bethke, Barrio Minton, Fernando, & O'Callaghan, 2010; Wesley, Minatreat and Watson, 2009; Cuijpers, Steunenberg, & Van Straten, 2007; King, 2007; Van der Weele, Gussekloo, De Waal, De Craen, & Van der Mast, 2008; Risley-Curtiss, 2010; Holley, & Wolf, 2006; Netting, Wilson, & New, 1987) as well as pre-coding and coding processes, themes are identified and include *visit/interaction* (Research Question 1), *acceptance* (Research Question 2), and *exposure /education*

(Research Question 3). The researcher presents an interpretation of findings with detailed discussions as well as table and figures to demonstrate how responses confirm and extend the knowledge base surrounding each of the research questions that guided this phenomenological, qualitative study. The methodological and executions limitations of the study are presented. This chapter concludes with recommendations for future research and potential positive social change implications.

## Overview of the Study

The beliefs, experiences, perspectives, and observations of 18 registered handlers who volunteered their animal therapy services in New York State were surveyed. Respondents were selected as a purposive, homogenous sample. The purpose of the study was to explore and better understand reasons for utilizing this service primarily in institutional settings, potential

barriers in transitioning to community-based settings,

and the prospective willingness of handlers to volunteer

their services in community locations. These concepts

are stated in detail as the research questions for this

study:

1.      Which attributes of institutional settings (i.e.

        nursing homes, hospitals, rehabilitation facilities)

        assist in the utilization of registered handler-

        animal therapy practices?

2.      What barriers may exist in transitioning registered

        handler-animal therapy practices to community

        settings (i.e. in home services, senior centers,

        adult day care programs)?

3.      How willing are registered handlers to practice in

        community settings?

Data was collected through a one-time electronic survey consisting of six, closed-ended questions, and 13 open-ended questions. Telephone interview data were collected from five respondents selected randomly from the group of 18 respondents, consisting of 10 open-ended questions. Survey and interview questions were designed to explore the lived experiences of a registered handler. The choice of a phenomenological approach for this qualitative study allowed for in-depth inquiry and description to better understand the identified phenomenon of registered handler-animal therapy. Key findings among survey respondents and interviewees included the themes of visit/interaction, acceptance, and exposure/education in relation to the research questions that guided this study.

## Interpretation of Findings

The data collection measurement tool used for this study was a self-created questionnaire consisting of six closed-ended questions and 13 open-ended questions, as well as follow up telephone interviews consisting of 10 open-ended questions guided by the phenomenon of registered handler-animal therapy, and the three research questions of this study. The research questions listed by number, focus area, and data gathering measurement tool are provided in Table 1.

*Table 1.* - Illustration of the Research Questions and their Data Gathering Instrument

| Research Question / Focus Area | Questionnaire Questions | Interview Questions |
|---|---|---|
| Attributes of Institutional Settings | 8, 9, 10, 11 | 3, 4, 5 |
| Barriers in Transitioning to Community Settings | 12, 15, 16, 18 | 2, 6, 7 |
| Willingness to Practice in Community Settings | 13, 14, 17, 19 | 8, 9, 10 |

## Research Question 1

Which attributes of institutional settings (i.e. nursing homes, hospitals, rehabilitation facilities) assist in the utilization of registered handler-animal therapy practices?

In this study, an institutional setting referred to a facility where individuals were given inpatient status characterized by having 24-hour care while living at a specific facility location. In contrast, a community setting referred to an environment where individuals were considered outpatient and services provided varied based on individual needs (McCall, 2001).

Respondents of this study confirmed this adaptation of animal-assisted therapy was consistently provided in hospitals, rehabilitation centers, nursing homes, and specialized care facilities (King 2007; Kramer et al., 2009). Respondents also confirmed the targeted populations to receive registered handler-animal therapy visits included children, adults, and older

adults diagnosed with chronic mental or health

conditions (Cuijpers et al., 2007; Friesen, 2009; Van der

Weele et al., 2008).

Lastly, respondents also confirmed the use of a

canine as a therapy animal was beneficial and provided

clients an object to interact with during visits and the

registered handler served as facilitator during

interactions. Respondents reported observations of a

positive change in client's mood and attitude as a result

of canine display of love and acceptance through visits

and interactions as indicated in the literature (Cuijpers et

al., 2007; Van der Weele et al., 2008). The concept of

registered handler-animal therapy is illustrated in Figure

3.

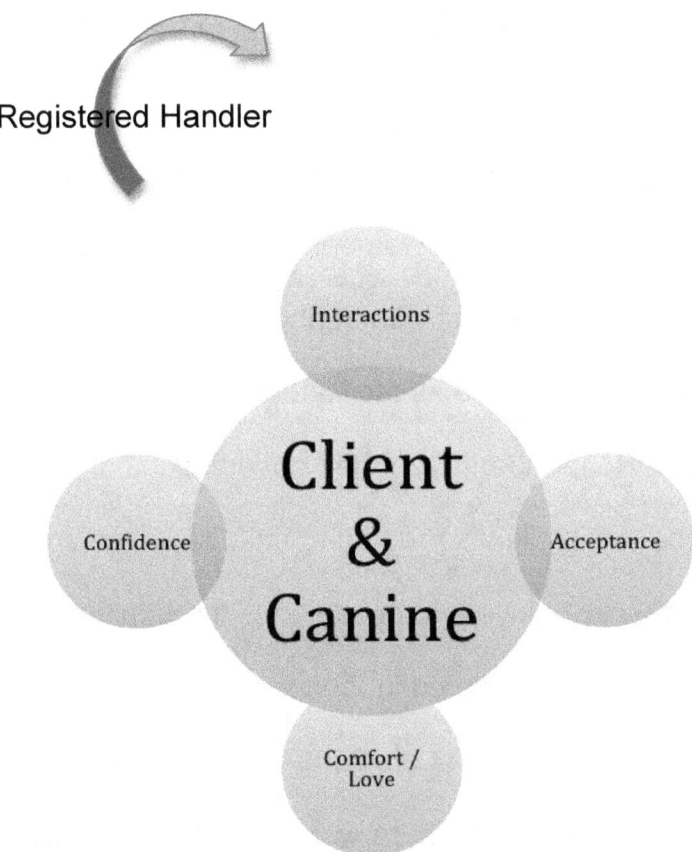

*Figure 3*. Illustration of the concept registered animal handler therapy.

## Research Question 2

What barriers may exist in transitioning registered handler-animal therapy practices to community settings (i.e. in home services, senior centers, adult day care programs)?

In Chapter 2, barriers to community care were discussed from a conceptual and organizational standpoint. Conceptually, there have been contradicting norms and expectations of older adults in the United States in terms of their abilities to maintain independence in the community, otherwise termed as *ageism* (Dallaire et al., 2008; Hudson, 2010). Respondents disconfirmed this concept and extended knowledge in this area in that barriers in transitioning registered handler-animal visits to community settings were environmental rather than client related. Respondents reported barriers to consider included scheduling, transportation, parking, and unfamiliar floor

plans that existed among community settings. From an

organizational standpoint, barriers related to community

care pertained to lack of awareness of various services,

including registered handler-animal practices resulting in

an under-utilization of community-based services

(Dallaire et al., 2008; Kane & Cutler, 2009; Tang &

Pickard, 2008). Moreover, for Behling et al. (2011),

administrative concerns coupled with being unfamiliar

with AAT practices in general have limited service

expansion. Respondents confirmed these barriers

existed and reported a desire for acceptance as well as

involvement of staff members during visits. Respondents

also reported a desire for a facilitator or supervisor to be

identified so communications related to registered

handler-animal therapy visits could be streamlined.

When asked for recommendations to transition

registered handler-animal therapy to community-based

settings, respondents reported the need for positive

media exposure and public education to increase

recruitment of volunteers so there would be available

registered teams to visit sites and locations regularly. In

spite of these barriers, respondents reported having a

positive outlook on their role as a registered handler.


## Research Question 3

How willing are registered handlers to practice in

community settings?

The secondary goal of this study was to

determine the prospective willingness of registered

handlers to practice in community settings as responses

could provide the feedback necessary to integrate this

service into existing community-based infrastructures to

assist in the expansion of animal therapy programs.

Researchers asserted there has been an inadequate

number of medical and social service professionals to

meet the needs of a growing older adult population

(Lehning & Austin, 2010; Salau, Rumbold, & Young,

2007; Stevenson, McRae, & Mughal, 2008; Wilson, et

al., 2008). Registered handlers volunteer their time to

provide animal therapy visits to a variety of client

populations in a range of settings, making them a viable

option in service planning for clients. Respondents

confirmed this and reported being willing to practice in

community settings, which aligned with the conceptual

and theoretical frameworks of this study.


## Conceptual Framework


The concept of the human-companion animal

bond (HCAB) is grounded in social work practice and

was used to guide this study. For Netting, Wilson, & New

(1987), the HCAB explores the person environment

concept and human experiences. The term *companion* is

associated with a psychological and emotional

attachment that has been the foundation for human

service professionals and researchers of animal-assisted

activities and animal-assisted therapy (Beck & Katcher,

2003; Horowitz, 2008; Walsh, 2009). Respondents

confirmed the human-companion animal bond concept

and reported observations of how registered handler-

animal visits and interactions had fostered rapport

building with clients and caregivers managing a chronic

condition. The rapport building aspect can also be

applied to the theoretical frameworks of this study.

**Theoretical Frameworks: Tönnies' *Gemeinschaft***
**and *Gesellschaft* and Durkheim's Mechanic**
**and Organic Solidarity**

For Tönnies (2001), the *Gemeinschaft* model of

community is characteristic of solidarity and shared

interpersonal relationships. Leadership, respect, and

care of members were a communal responsibility (Haidt

& Graham, 2009; Mellow, 2005). Similarly, Durkheim

(1965) characterized mechanic solidarity as "bonds of

blood" (p. 432) in which members share responsibilities

for the livelihood of the community. In this study,

respondents confirmed the significance of community

care and its potential impact on the older adult

population. Moreover, a majority of respondents reported

being willing to practice in community-based settings

demonstrating that shared interpersonal relationships

were desired.

The *Gesellschaft* model of society prioritized

individual needs and ambitions, thus weakening

interpersonal bonds (Kamenka, 1965; Mellow, 2005;

Tönnies, 2001). Similarly, Durkheim (1947) focused on

the autonomy of individuals in the notion of organic

solidarity. This autonomy has resulted in a complex

society comprised of specific tasks, otherwise termed as

division of labor (Dew, 2007). In this study, respondents

extended this knowledge to contemporary society in

which institutional settings are separate and distinct in

providing client care and support, indicative of bonding
and bridging social capital.

Researchers characterized bonding social capital
as a reiterative interaction in which a form of assistance
is provided among individuals. In contrast, bridging
social capital refers to a social organization in order to
access communal resources (Collum, 2008).

Researchers asserted bonding and bridging
social capital does foster trust and engagement among
people (Collum, 2008; Hawkins & Maurer, 2012; Keating
& Dosman, 2009). In this study, respondents confirmed
and extended this knowledge as the need for interaction
has remained. Moreover, the scope has broadened to
include interactions from humans and animals that can
involve physical and emotional tasks to promote
individual well-being as illustrated in Figure 4.

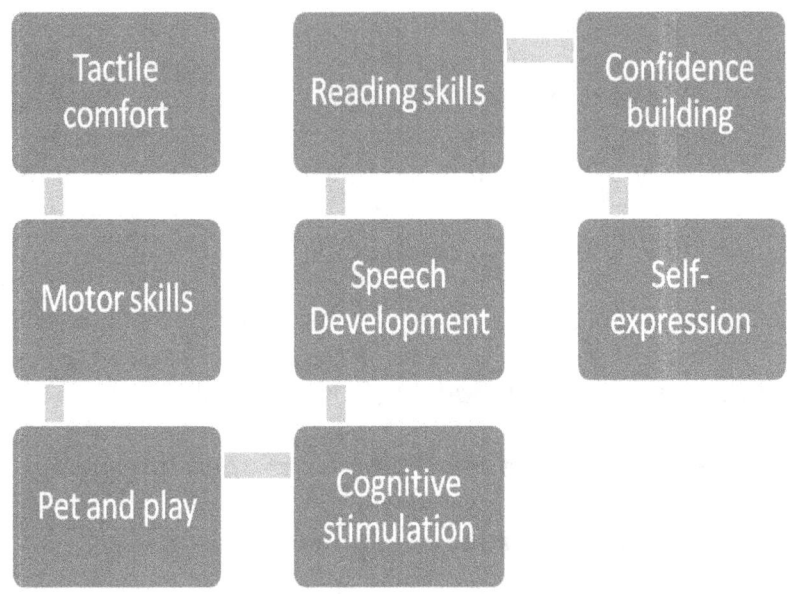

*Figure 3 - Illustration of Registered Handler-Animal Therapy Interactions.*

## Limitations and Recommendations

As discussed in Chapters 1 and 4, there were limitations of this study that required attention. In terms of methodology limitations, the purposive, homogenous sampling strategy of this study and the number of respondents (18) who participated limited the generalizability of the research findings. Individuals who were recruited for this study were registered handlers of a specific age range, and resided or volunteered in New York State. These criteria limited the type of experiences and perspectives of therapy animal practices in other geographical areas. It is recommended that additional research with a larger, heterogeneous sample targeted throughout the United States be conducted to allow a generalization of study findings (Le Roux & Kemp, 2009).

The use of a self created questionnaire and follow-up telephone interviews for the collection of data allowed for the exploration of perspectives and attitudes, intended to enhance understanding for evaluative purposes. Using a self-created questionnaire also required careful consideration in terms of bias, which is discussed in Chapters 3 and 4. It is recommended for future research efforts, pre-existing measurement tools within a mixed methods design be utilized to assert a more extensive strategy of evaluation (Behling et al.,

2011). There were also limitations in regards to the

execution of the study that require consideration.

The first limitation to consider was the potential

for discrepant cases for analysis as all 18 respondents

did not complete each question of the questionnaire. The

second limitation included the unequal distribution of

demographics in terms of the gender and ages of the

study participants, which had the potential to result in

skewed responses. A third limitation included the state of

the written responses, as there were grammatical and

spelling errors as well as incomplete sentences present.

Similarly, transcription of the telephone interviews using

the audio files proved to be difficult. Due to variations in

sound quality, tone, and speech of the interviewee,

transcript content may have been altered compared to

the content of the verbal conversation. A measurement

tool is recommended for data collection utilization among

a large sample size for future research efforts. (Risley-

Curtiss, 2010).

## Reflection on Study and Findings

The planning, implementation, and analysis process

involved in this research study confirmed the

researchers choice of a qualitative design. While

numerical research exists on the impact of animal-

assisted therapy, there is a lack of knowledge pertaining

to the individuals who provide this service. Participants

of this research study reported feeling validated and

encouraged by this study. Participants also reported

their desire for systemic change (recruitment efforts,

media exposure, additional volunteer/visitation

opportunities, supervision at locations) based on study

findings, which was surprising to the researcher. Coming

from a social work background and a client focused

training, the researcher presumed participants would

primarily provide experiences related to client

interactions. While specific client stories were reported,

participants linked these direct practice experiences to

their desires for systemic and program related changes.

Acknowledging this study finding, if time and resources

were infinite, the researcher would have implemented a

qualitative, focus group study. For Patton (2002), a focus

group is an interview with a group of people for

approximately one to two hours in which the information

gathered is based on the questions provided by the

researcher ,but also the physical setting and interactions

of participants. In this study, the primary measurement

tool was a self-created survey, distributed electronically.

The secondary tool included follow-up telephone

interviews. The selection of these measurement tools

was appropriate given varied geographical locations and

unknown schedules of participants, but it did eliminate

face-to-face interactions that could have provided an

additional path of inquiry. In spite of these limitations, the

findings of this study can add to the existing knowledge

base for human service professionals and have the

potential to impact social change.

Photo courtesy of author

## Social Change Implications

The primary goal of this empirical phenomenological study was to explore the perspectives, attitudes, beliefs and experiences of registered handler-animal therapy volunteers in New York State on transitioning this intervention from institutional facilities to include community-based environments. The level of cooperation from the agency partner, the receptiveness towards the recruitment and informed consent process from potential participants as well as the willingness of the respondents who completed the electronic questionnaire and who participated in a follow up telephone interview exceeded my expectations and resulted in a content rich data analysis process.

The secondary goal of this study was to assess prospectively how willing registered handler-animal therapy volunteers are to practicing in community-based settings. The discussions in Chapters 4 and 5 have demonstrated respondents are willing to provide registered handler-animal therapy services in community locations, with insight into the barriers that exist from an organizational standpoint. With this information, it is possible collaborative efforts can be mobilized to address these barriers. If action steps can be done, a dialogue with New York City's Department of the Aging and the community based case management agencies can take place. Ideally, with study findings, case management agencies will consider integrating registered handler-animal therapy services (program modification) into existing service care plans or establishing programs in under-developed case management agencies (program development) in hopes of meeting the needs of older adults' aging in place in New York State.

It is estimated individuals, aged 65 and older, will

double to 70 million by the year 2030 in the United

States (Masotti, Fick, Johnson-Masotti, & MacLeod,

2006). Moreover, the number of older adults choosing to

remain in their homes and communities as they age is

increasing (Scharlach, 2009b). With a growing aging

demographic, there is a need for alternatives to inpatient

care that is cost effective and community-based, which

arguably, is striving for positive social change. According

to Brilliant (2013), "Social change is participatory. That's

what makes it social. It has always required intellectual

and moral catalysts. But lasting change happens by

engaging and affecting large numbers of people" (p.26).

In pursuit of the goals of this research study, contact with

the agency partner was initiated two years ago and has

been actively maintained for the duration of the study

and the researcher speculates, communication will

continue in the future. The involvement of the agency

partner was critical in the completion of this research

study, from understanding the multifaceted aspects of

registered handler-animal therapy to supporting dissemination of study findings. In addition, with these research findings, it is possible this volunteer-based service will pursue certification and/or licensure to promote the integrity and professionalism in the field of animal-assisted therapy. As such, it is a personal goal this research study be the foundation for future studies in an attempt to mobilize administration and leadership efforts within the human services profession and animal therapy field to meet the emotional needs of all client populations.

# REFERENCES

Alley, D., Liebig, P., Pynoos, J., Banerjee, T., & Choi, I. (2007). Creating elder-friendly communities: Preparations for an aging society. *Journal of Gerontological Social Work*, *49*(1-2), 1-18.

American Art Therapy Association. (2012) Art therapy: Definition of the profession. (2012). Retrieved from http://www.americanarttherapyassociation.org/aata-aboutus.html

American Art Therapy Association. (2012). Art therapy (2012). Retrieved from http://www.americanarttherapyassociation.org/aata-aboutus.html

American Music Therapy Association. (2011). History of music therapy. (2011). Retrieved from http://www.musictherapy.org/about/history/

American Music Therapy Association. (2006). American music therapy association, inc. Retrieved from http://www.musictherapy.org/assets/1/7/MT_Alzheimers_2006.pdf

American Music Therapy Association. (2011). What is music therapy? (2011). Retrieved from http://www.musictherapy.org/about/quotes/

Beard, J. R., Cerda, M., Blaney, S., Ahern, J., Vlahov, D., & Galea, S. (2009). Neighborhood characteristics and change in depressive symptoms among older residents of New York City. *American Journal of Public Health*, *99*(7), 1308-1314.

Beck, A. M., & Katcher, A. H. (2003). Future directions in human-animal bond research. *American Behavioral Scientist*, *47*(1), 79-93.

Behling, R. J., Haefner, J., & Stowe, M. (2011). Animal programs and animal-assisted in Illinois long-term care facilities twenty years later (1990-2010). *Academy of Health Care Management Journal,*, 7, 109-117.

Black, K. (2008). Health and aging in place: Implications for community practice. *Journal of Community Practice*, *16*(1), 79-95.

Bookman, A. (2008). Innovative models of aging in place: Transforming our communities for an aging population. *Community, Work & Family*, *11*(4), 419-438. doi:10.1080/13668800802362334.

Brilliant, L. (2013). Fifty years of social change. *Stanford Social Innovation Review, 11*(2), 26-28.

Cannuscio, C., Block, J., & Kawachi, I. (2003). Social capital and successful aging: The role of senior housing. *Annals of Internal Medicine, 139.* 395-399.

Castle, N., Ferguson, J., & Schulz, R. (2009). Aging friendly health and long-term-care services. *Generations*, *33*(2), 44-50.

Chandler, C. K., Portrie-Bethke, T. L., Barrio Minton, C. A., Fernando, D. M., & O'Callaghan, D. M. (2010). Matching animal-assisted therapy techniques and intentions with counseling guiding theories. *Journal of Mental Health Counseling, 32*(4), 354-374.

Cohen-Mansfield, J., & Frank, J. . (2008). Relationship between perceived needs and assessed needs for services in community-dwelling older persons. *The Gerontologist, 48*(4), 505-16. doi: 1552987371.

Collom, E. (2008). Engagement of the elderly in time banking: The potential for social capital generation in an aging society. *Journal of Aging & Social Policy, 20*(4), 414-436.

Connell, C. M., Janevic, M. R., Solway, E., & McLaughlin, S. J. (2007). Are pets a source of support or added burden for married couples facing dementia? *Journal of Applied Gerontology, 26*(5), 472-485.

Creswell, J. W. (2009). *Research design: Qualitative, quantitative, and mixed method approaches. (3rd edition).* Thousand Oaks, CA: SAGE Publications.

Creswell, J.W. (2007). *Qualitative inquiry and research design: Choosing among the five approaches. (2$^{nd}$ edition).* Thousand Oaks, CA: SAGE Publications.

Cuijpers, P., Steunenberg, B., & Van Straten, A. (2007). Actions taken to cope with depressed mood: The role of personality traits. *Aging & Mental Health, 11*(4), 457-463.

Dallaire, B., McCubbin, M., Carpenter, N., & Clement, M. (2008). Representations of elderly with mental health problems held by psychosocial practitioners from community and institutional settings. *Social Work in Mental Health, 7*, 139-152.

Dew, K. (2007). Public health and the cult of humanity: A neglected Durkheimian concept. *Sociology of Health & Illness, 29*(1), 100-114.

Durkheim, E. (1947). *The division of labor in society.* Glencoe, IL: Free Press.

Durkheim, E. (1960). *The rules of sociological method.* New York, NY: Free Press.

Durkheim, E. (1965). *The elementary forms of the religious life.* New York, NY: Oxford University Press.

Durkheim, E. (2007). *On suicide.* London, England: Penguin Classics.

Dyer, C., Pickens, S., & Burnett, J. (2007). Vulnerable elders: When it is no longer safe to live alone. *The Journal of the American Medical Association, 298*(12), 1448-1450.

Everingham, J., Petriwskji, A., Warburton, J., Cuthill, M., & Bartlett, H. (2009). Information provision for an age-friendly community. *Ageing International, 34,* 79-98. doi: 10.1007/s12126-009-9036-5.

Friesen, L. (2010). Exploring animal-assisted programs with children in school. *Early Childhood Education Journal, 37*, 261-267. doi:10.1007/s10643-009-0349-5

Gonzalez, P. (2011). The impact of music therapists' music cultures on the development of their professional frameworks. *Qualitative Inquiries in Music Therapy, 6*, 1-33.

Graves, J. (2007). Factors influencing indirect speech and language therapy interventions for adults with learning disabilities: The perceptions of carers and therapists. *International Journal of Language and Communication Disorders, 42*(1), 103-121.

Haidt, J., & Graham, J. (2009). Planet of the Durkheimians, where community, authority, and sacredness are foundations of morality. *Social and Psychological Bases of Ideology and System Justification* (pp. 371-401). New York, NY: Oxford University Press.

Hansen, J. C. (2008). Community and in home models. *Journal of Social Work Education, 44*(3), 83-87.

Hawkins, R. & Maurer, K. (2012). Unravelling social capital: Disentangling a concept for social work. *British Journal of Social Work, 42.* 353-370.

Holmqvist, K., Kamwendo, K., & Ivarsson, A. B. (2009). Occupational therapists' descriptions of their work with persons suffering from cognitive impairment following acquired brain injury. *Scandinavian Journal of Occupational Therapy, 16,* 13-24.

Horowitz, S. (2008). The human-animal bond: Health implications across the lifespan. *Alternative and Complementary Therapies, 14*(5), 251-256.

Hudson, R. B. (2010). Analysis and advocacy in home-and community-based care: An approach in three parts. *Journal of Gerontological Social Work, 53,* 3-20.

Inglis, D. (2009). Cosmopolitan sociology and the classical canon: Ferdinand Tönnies and the emergence of global Gesellschaft. *British Journal of Sociology, 60*(4), 813-832. doi:10.1111/j.1468-4446.2009.01276.x.

Jasperson, R. (2010). Animal-assisted therapy with female inmates with mental illness: A case example from a pilot program. *Journal of Offender Rehabilitation, 49,* 417-433. doi:10.1080/10509674.2010.499056

Kamenka, E. (1965). Gemeinschaft and Gesellschaft. *Political Science, 17*(3), 3-12.

Kane, R. A., & Cutler, L. J. (2009). Promoting homeline characteristics and eliminating institutional characteristics in community-based residental care settings: Insights from an 8-state study. *Seniors Housing & Care Journal, 17*(1), 16-37.

Kawamura, N., Niiyama, M., & Niiyama, H. (2007). Long-term evaluation of animal-assisted therapy for institutionalized elderly people: A preliminary result. *Psychogeriatrics, 7*(1), 8-13. doi:10.1111/j.1479-8301.2006.00156.x

Keating, N. & Dosman, D. (2009). Social capital and the care networks of frail seniors. *Canadian Sociological Association, 46*(4), 302-318.

Kelly, J. (2010). What is art therapy and how do we know it works? An Australian perspective on the need for more research. *The International Journal of Interdisciplinary Social Sciences, 5,* 256-259.

King, L. (2007). *Animal-assisted therapy: A guide for professional counselors, school counselors, social workers, and educators.* Bloomington, IN: Author House.

Kramer, S. C., Friedman, E., & Bernstein, P. L. (2009). Comparison of the effect of human interaction, animal-assisted therapy, and AIBO-assisted therapy on long-term care residents with dementia. *Anthrozoos, 22*(1), 43-57.

Le Roux, M. C., & Kemp, R. (2009). Effect of a companion dog on depression and anxiety levels of elderly residents in a long-term care facility. *Psychogeriatrics, 9,* 23-26. doi:10.1111/j.1479-8301.2009.00268.x

Lehning, A. A., & Austin, M. J. (2010). Long-term care in the United States: Policy themes and promising practices. *Journal of Gerontological Social Work, 53,* 43-63.

Lockhart, C., Giles-Sims, J., & Klopfenstein, K. (2009). Comparing states Medicaid nursing facilities and home and community-based services long-term care programs: Quality and fit with inclination, capacity, and need. *Journal of Aging & Social Policy, 21,* 52-74.

Macauley, B. L. (2006). Animal-assisted therapy for persons with aphasia: A pilot study. *Journal of Rehabilitation Research & Development, 43*(3), 357-365.

Masotti, P. J., Fick, R., Johnson-Masotti, A., & MacLeod, S. (2006). Healthy naturally occurring retirement communities: A low-cost approach to facilitating health aging. *Community Matters in Health Aging, 96*(7), 1164-1170.

McCall, N. (2001) Long term care: Definition, demand, cost, and financing. In N. McCall (Ed.), *Who will pay for long-term care,* Chicago, IL: Health Administration Press

McCluskey, A., & Middleton, S. (2010). Increasing delivery of an outdoor journey intervention to people with stroke: A feasibility study involving five community rehabilitation teams. *Implementation Science, 5*(59), 1-10.

Mellow, M. (2005). The work of rural professionals: Doing the Gemeinschaft-Gesellschaft gavotte. *Rural Sociology, 70*(1), 50-69. doi:817641381.

Moustakas, C. (1994). *Phenomenological research methods.* Thousand Oaks, CA: SAGE Publications.

Nancarrow, S. A., Moran, A. M., & Parker, S. G. (2009). Understanding service context: Development of a service pro forma to describe and measure elderly peoples' community and intermediate care services. *Health and Social Care in the Community, 17*(5), 434-446.

National PACE Association. (2002) Where is PACE? (2002). Retrieved from http://www.npaonline.org/custom/programsearch.asp?id=209

National PACE Association. (2002). Who, what and where is PACE? Retrieved from http://www.npaonline.org/website/article.asp?id=12#History

Netting, F. E., Wilson, C. C., & New, J. C. (1987, January). The human-animal bond: Implications for practice. *National Association of Social Workers, Inc.,* 60-64.

New York City Department for the Aging. (2012). Census 2010: Changes in the elderly population of New York City, 2000-2010. Retrieved from http://www.nyc.gov/html/dfta/downloads/pdf/demographic/elderly_population_070912.pdfRetrieved from http://www.nyc.gov/html/dfta/html/home/home.shtml

O'Grady, L., & McFerran, K. (2007). Community music therapy and its relationship to community music: Where does it end? *Nordic Journal of Music Therapy, 16*(1), 14-26.

Older Americans Act of 1965, Pub. L. No. 109-365, § 1 (2006). Retrieved
  http://www.aoa.gov/AOA_programs/OAA/oaa_full.asp
Patton, M.Q. (2002). *Qualitative research & evaluation methods. (3^{rd} ed.).*
  Thousand Oaks, CA: SAGE Publications.
Pennington, J., & Knight, T. (2008). Staying connected: The lived
  experiences of volunteers and older adults. *Ageing International, 32,*
  298-311. doi: 10.007/s12126-009-9036-5.
Pickering, W. (2008). Emile Durkheim. In J. Corrigan (Ed.), *The Oxford
  handbook of religion and emotion* (pp. 438-456). New York,
  NY:Oxford University Press.
Pickering, W., & Walford, G. (2000). *Durkheim's suicide: A century of
  research and debate.* London: Routledge.
Pierini, D., & Volker, D. (2009). Living alone in community and over 85
  years old: A case study. *Southern Online Journal of Nursing
  Research, 9*(1).
Prus, R. (2009). Reconceptualizing the study of community life. *American
  Sociologist, 40*(1/2), 106-146. doi:10.1007/s12108-009-9066-1.
Putnam, R.D. (1993). The prosperous community. *The American Project,
  4*(13), 1-11.
Pynoos, J., Caraviello, R., & Cicero, C. (2009). Lifelong housing: The
  anchor in aging friendly communities. *Generations, 33*(2), 26-32.
Quick, L., Harman, S., Morgan, S., & Stagnitti, K. (2010). Scope of practice
  of occupational therapists working in Victorian community health
  settings. *Australian Occupational Therapy Journal, 57,* 95-101.
Rhee, Y., Degenholtz, H. B., Lo Sasso, A. T., & Emanuel, L. L. (2009).
  Estimating the quantity and economic value of family caregiving for
  community-dwelling older persons in the last year. *The American
  Geriatrics Society, 5,* 1654-1659.
Risley-Curtiss, C. (2010, January). Social work practitioners and the
  human-companion animal bond: A national study. *Social Work, 55*(1),
  38-46.
Risley-Curtiss, C., Holley, L. C., & Wolf, S. (2006). The animal-human bond
  and ethnic diversity. *Social Work, 51*(3), 257-268.
Salau, S., Rumbold, B., & Young, B. (2007). From concept to care:
  Enabling community care through a health promoting palliative care
  approach. *Contempory Nurse, 27,* 132-140.
Saldaña, J. (2009). *The coding manual for qualitative researchers.*
  Thousand Oaks, CA: SAGE Publications.
Scharlach, A. (2009a). Frameworks for fostering aging friendly community
  change. *Generations, 33*(2), 71-73.
Scharlach, A. (2009b). Creating aging friendly communities: Why America's
  cities and towns must become better places to grow. *Generations,
  33*(2), 5-11.
Souter, M. A., & Miller, M. D. (2007). Do animal-assisted activities
  effectively treat depression? A meta-analysis. *Anthrozoos, 20*(2), 167-
  180. doi:10.2752/175303707X207954
Stevenson, L., McRae, C., & Mughal, W. (2008). Moving to a culture of
  safety in community home health care. *Journal of Health Services
  Research & Policy, 13*(1), 20-24.

Sweeney, S. (2009). Art therapy: Promoting well-being in rural and remote communities. *Australian Psychiatry, 17*, 152-154.

Tang, F., & Pickard, J. G. (2008). Aging in place or relocation: Perceived awareness of community-based long-term care and services. *Journal of Housing for the Elderly, 22*(4), 404-422.

The American Occupation Therapy Association, Inc. (2012) What is occupational therapy? (2012). Retrieved from http://www.aota.org/Consumers.aspx

Tönnies, F. (2001). *Community and civil society.* Cambridge: Cambridge University Press.

Tsai, C. C., Friedmann, E., & Thomas, S. A. (2010). The effect of animal-assisted therapy on stress responses in hospitalized children. *Anthrozoös, 23*(3), 245-258. doi:10.2752/175303710X12750451258977

U.S. Census Bureau: Population Division (2001). Sixty-five plus in the United States. Retrieved from http://www.census.gov/population/socdemo/statbriefs/agebrief.html

Van der Weele, G. M., Gussekloo, J., De Waal, M. W., De Craen, A. J., & Van der Mast, R. C. (2008). Co-occurrence of depression and anxiety in elderly subjects aged 90 years and its relationship with functional status, quality of life and mortality. *International Journal of Geriatric Psychiatry, 24*, 595-601.

Villalta-Gil, V. V., Roca, M., Gonzalez, N., Cuca, E., Escanilla, A., Asensio, M. R., & Esteban, M. E. (2009). Dog-assisted therapy in the treatment of chronic schizophrenic inpatients. *Anthrozoös, 22*(2), 149-159. doi:10.2752/175303709X434176

Walsh, F. (2009). Human-animal bonds I: The relational significance of companion animals. *Family Process, 48*(4), 462-480.

Wesley, M. C., Minatra, N. B., & Watson, J. C. (2009). Animal-assisted therapy in the treatment of substance dependence. *Anthrozoös, 22*(2), 137-148. doi:10.2752/175303709X434167

Williams, E., & Jenkins, R. (2008). Dog visitation therapy in dementia care: A literature review. *Nursing Older People, 20*(8), 31-35.

Williams, H. G., Ullmann, G., Gossard, J. L., Hussey, J. R., Brotherton, S. S., Laditka, J., & Cornman, C. (2009). Functional status assessment for community long-term care: Preliminary observations. *Home Health Care Services Quarterly, 28*, 151-171.

Wilson, D. M., Ross, C., Goodridge, D., Davis, P., Landreville, A., & Roebuck, K. (2008). The care needs of community-dwelling seniors suffering from advanced chronic obstructive pulmonary disease. *Canadian Journal on Aging, 24*(4), 347-357.

Wood, L., Giles-Corti, B., & Bulsara, M. (2005). The pet connection: Pets as a conduit for social capital? *Social Science $ Medicine, 61.* 1159-1173.

Yarmo-Roberts, D., Freak-Poli, R. L., Cooper, B., Noonan, T., Stolewinder, J., & Reid, C. M. (2010). The heart of the matter: Health status of aged care clients receiving home- and community-based care. *Journal of Aging Research*, 1-6.

Yong, F. (2007). The Olmstead decision and the journey toward integration:

The evolution of social work responses. *Journal of Gerontological Social Work, 49*(1/2), 115-126.

# APPENDIX A

## Research Study Questionnaire
*(Transitioning Registered Handler-Animal Therapy from the Institution to the Community)*

## PLEASE ANSWER THE FOLLOWING QUESTIONS ABOUT YOURSELF

NOTE: The term "institutional setting" refers to in-patient facilities used by older adults, including but not limited to: nursing homes, rehabilitation centers, hospitals, and hospices. The term "community setting" refers to out-patient services including but not limited to: in-home programs, senior centers, and adult day-care programs.

1. How old are you?
   - Younger than18 years old
   - 18-21 years old
   - 22-25 years old
   - 26-30 years old
   - 31-35 years old
   - 36-40 years old
   - Older than 41 years old

2. What is your gender?
   - Male
   - Female
   - Prefer not to answer

3. Are you a registered handler?
   - Yes

- o No
- o Prefer not to answer

4. Would you be willing to participate in a follow-up telephone interview?
- o Yes, my preferred contact number is _____
- o No
- o Prefer not to answer

5. How long have you worked as a registered handler?
- o Less than 1 year
- o 1-3 years
- o 4-6 years
- o 7-10 years
- o 11-15 years
- o 16-18 years
- o 19-20 years

6. Do you use a canine as the primary therapy animal?
- o Yes
- o No

If "yes" proceed to question 7. If "no," proceed to question 13.

7. What breed(s) of canine do you work with when conducting sessions?

8. How is the canine utilized in handler-animal interactions? Explain.

9. In what types of facilities/institutions have you practiced handler-animal interactions with a canine (i.e. nursing homes, hospitals, hospices)?

10. In these facilities and institutions, what populations have you worked with (i.e. children, adults, elderly,

diagnosis of chronic mental or health condition)?

11. In your opinion, what are the benefits, if any, of using a canine as a therapy animal? Explain.

12. In your opinion, what are the concerns, if any, of using a canine as a therapy animal? Explain.

13. How would you describe the purpose of handler-animal interactions?

14. Do you think that providing handler-animal services at the community level would be beneficial (i.e. in home programs, senior centers, adult day programs)? Explain.

15. What would be the difficulties involved in providing handler-animal services in community settings? Explain.

16. What modifications to handler-animal interactions do you recommend for community level services? Explain.

17. In your opinion, what aspects of community level handler-animal interactions would help expand this service? Explain.

18. In your opinion, what aspects of community level handler-animal interactions would limit this service? Explain.

19. How willing would you be to practice in community settings? Explain.

# APPENDIX B

## *Transitioning Registered Handler-Animal Therapy from the Institution to the Community*

## Interview Script

Thank you for taking the time out of your busy schedule to speak with me today. I am very excited to be working on my dissertation at Walden University and have a deep passion for social services and all service delivery programs. At Walden University, all PhD students must complete a research project demonstrating abilities to collaborate, create and implement a research design, as well as collect and analyze the data.

I am speaking with you today to ask you 10 questions about your experiences as a registered handler. These questions were reviewed and approved by my research supervisor and approved by the Walden IRB board as being little to no risk of harm to participants. In addition, I have the consent form that you provided an electronic signature. As a reminder, all information is confidential and your participation is voluntary. If at any time, you feel uncomfortable or do not wish to continue this phone interview, please tell me. Do you have any questions at this time? <Allow time for participant to respond>

Ok, thank you. Let's get started!

**Q1.** *[Mini Tour/Historical Experience – historical baseline for comparative analysis across other questions]* As you may know, participating in a follow-up interview was not a requirement to be involved in this research study. I appreciate your cooperation in this regard and would like to start by discussing your decision to participate in a follow-up interview. What are some reasons why you chose to a follow-up interviewee?

**Q2.** *[Hypothetical Question to explore needs and desires]* In qualitative interviewing, asking a hypothetical question is an excellent approach to exploring how you would handle a situation or what your hopes for a situation would be. Therefore, if you could change just one thing about your current practices in terms of how a canine is used in registered-handler interventions, what would it be?

**Q3.** *[Assessing Registered Handler-Animal Practices: General]* Based on your experiences as a registered handler-animal therapy team, how would you describe the purpose of this service? Please specify the locations in which you volunteer as well.

**Q4.** *[Assessing Registered Handler-Animal Practices: Focused]* As we just discussed, there are a variety of institutional settings in which services are provided. Can you share some of your experiences when working in these environments, whether positive or negative?

**Q5.** *[Meaning of Word; comparative]* It sounds like your services in these institutions are valuable. With interests in community-based work, I wonder if these services would be appropriate at that level. Before moving forward, can you define of both of these terms (*institutions* and *community*)?

**Q6.** *[Overall Outlook on Transition]* The transition of providing registered handler-animal therapy services from institutions to communities could be difficult in terms of establishing community partnerships and a client population. How does that make you feel?

**Q7.** *[Community-based Insights]* The rest of the questions in this interview will focus in the areas of community-based registered handler-animal therapy services. As you may know, registered handlers have different approaches when working with client populations, older adults in particular. What is your registered handler practices like when working with older adults?

**Q8.** *[Community-based Registered Handler-Animal Practices; Philosophical Domains; Hypothetical; Focused]* This may be a bit of a fun question to think about! If you were selected as the "model" registered handler and were asked to share with others your three biggest secrets on how to modify the program structure in order to serve more older adults in community-based settings, what would they be and why?

**Q9.** *[Community-based Registered Handler-Animal Practices; Difficult Practice Areas; Experience]* I would like to dig a little deeper on this topic. You are providing great insight! If additional registered handler-animal services were provided to additional community environments, particularly for older adults, how could this benefit and/or hinder this volunteer based program?

**Q10.** *[Community-based Registered Handler-Animal Practices; Successful Moments; Experience]* And finally, do you have an experience that you can share with me discussing how willing you may be to volunteer your services as a registered handler-animal therapy team in more community environments?

I want to thank you again for taking the time to discuss these questions with me today. Do you have any questions I can answer for? It has truly been a pleasure speaking with you today and thank you for participating in this research project.

# APPENDIX C

# CODEBOOK

| Questions #1-6: | Question # | Respondent # | Key Term Used | Code |
|---|---|---|---|---|
| Demographic | 8 | 2 | interaction | Attribute |
| | | 3 | interaction | Attribute |
| Question #7: | | 4 | accepting | Values / Theming |
| Breed of canine | | 5 | interacts | Attribute |
| | | 6 | visit | Attribute |
| Question #9: | | 13 | visit | Attribute |
| Type of institution | | 14 | visit | Attribute |
| | | 15 | visit | Attribute |
| Question #10: | | 16 | interaction | Attribute |
| Type of client population | | 17 | interact | Attribute |
| Question #12: | 11 | 1 | express | Values |
| Canine Concerns | | 2 | acceptance | Values / Theming |
| | | 3 | interaction | Attribute |
| | | 4 | acceptance | Values / |

| Questions #1-6: | Question # | Respondent # | Key Term Used | Code |
|---|---|---|---|---|
| | | | | Theming |
| | | 7 | interacting | Attribute |
| | | 11 | accepting | Values / Theming |
| | | 15 | accepting | Values / Theming |
| | 13 | 1 | trust and confidence | Values / Theming |
| | | 2 | interaction | Attribute |
| | | 3 | trust and love | Values / Theming |
| | | 4 | visit | Attribute |
| | | 5 | acceptance | Values / Theming |
| | | 7 | interactions | Attribute |
| | | 12 | love | Values / Theming |
| | | 13 | interaction | Attribute |
| | | 16 | visit | Attribute |
| | | 17 | love | Values / Theming |
| | | 18 | interact | Attribute |
| | 14 | 3 | visit | Attribute |
| | | 4 | visiting | Attribute |
| | | 5 | interaction | Attribute |
| | | 16 | visit | Attribute |
| | | 8 | visitation | Attribute |

| Questions #1-6: | Question # | Respondent # | Key Term Used | Code |
|---|---|---|---|---|
| | 15 | 11 | acceptance | Values / Theming |
| | | 15 | visit | Attribute |
| | | 16 | visit | Attribute |
| | 16 | 1 | education | Attribute |
| | | 2 | staff involvement | Attribute |
| | | 3 | representative | Attribute |
| | | 9 | match teams | Attribute |
| | | 10 | supervision | Attribute |
| | | 13 | small groups | Attribute |
| | | 15 | owner's responsibility | Attribute |
| | 17 | 1 | exposure | Attribute |
| | | 2 | education | Attribute |
| | | 3 | representative | Attribute |
| | | 4 | exposure | Attribute |
| | | 5 | exposure | Attribute |
| | | 6 | publicize | Attribute |
| | | 8 | exposure | Attribute |
| | | 9 | education | Attribute |
| | | 11 | marketing | Attribute |
| | | 13 | visited | Attribute |
| | | 14 | interactions | Attribute |
| | | 15 | education | Attribute |

| Questions #1-6: | Question # | Respondent # | Key Term Used | Code |
|---|---|---|---|---|
| | 18 | 4 | interaction | Attribute |
| | | 7 | visit | Attribute |
| | | 9 | visit | Attribute |
| | | 10 | visit | Attribute |
| | | 13 | interactions | Attribute |
| | | 14 | visit | Attribute |
| | | 15 | acceptance | Values / Theming |
| | 19 | 3 | visited | Attribute |
| | | 4 | visit | Attribute |
| | | 12 | visit | Attribute |

## Considerations/Typos/ Mechanical Errors

Q8, R# 5, 6, 16
Q11, R #4,5, 10, 16,
Q10, R# 4,5,11, 16
Q13, R# 5,6,7,12, 17
Q14, R#2,5,6,12,
Q15, R# 5,6,12
Q16, R# 5,6,7,
Q17, R#5,6,15
Q18, R# 3,5,6,16
Q19, R# 7,10,

# APPENDIX D

*Deepest gratitude to the organization **Pet Partners** for providing many of the photos used throughout the book to illustrate the research study.  Written permission to use these photos in the book has been obtained, on file, and available via both the author and the organization.*

## Pet Partners – The Organization

## ABOUT PET PARTNERS

Pet Partners is the nation's largest and most prestigious nonprofit registering handlers of multiple species as volunteer teams providing Animal-Assisted Interactions.   With the highest caliber curriculum in the industry, Pet Partners trains volunteers and evaluates them with their pets for visiting animal programs in hospitals, nursing homes, veterans' centers, hospice, Alzheimer's facilities, courtrooms, schools and other settings. We offer our teams superior risk management and the industry's highest safety standards, continuing education and re-registration and keen attention to dealing with our unique multi-species team population.

Pet Partners is the national leader in demonstrating and promoting positive human-animal therapy, activities and education. Nearly 40 years since the organization's inception, the science that proves these benefits has become indisputable. Today, Pet Partners is the nation's largest and most prestigious nonprofit registering handlers of multiple species as volunteer teams providing animal-assisted interactions.

Pet Partners teams interact with a wide variety of clients including: veterans with PTSD, seniors living with Alzheimer's, students with literacy challenges, patients in recovery, people with intellectual disabilities, and those approaching end of life. The impact of these interactions is felt one million times a year. Pet Partners' curriculum and continuing education for licensed instructors, evaluators, and handlers is the gold standard in the field.

People and animal volunteer teams are the heart and soul of Pet Partners' Therapy Animal Program. Therapy animals aren't just dogs. Cats, horses, rabbits, pigs, birds, llamas, alpacas, guinea pigs, and even rats are eligible for evaluation through the Pet Partners program.

1. Founded in 1977, Pet Partners is the leader in demonstrating and promoting positive human-animal therapy, activities, and education.

2. The Pet Partners Difference: superior risk management and highest industry safety standards, continuing education and re-registration for teams, and keen attention to dealing with our unique multi-species team population.

3. Pet Partners' teams visit hospitals, schools, nursing homes, VA Centers, and many other facilities across the country.

4. More than just dogs, other species of therapy animals include: cats, horses, birds, rabbits, and more,

5. Over 10,000 Pet Partners therapy animal teams in 48 states. Last year, Pet Partners teams made 1,000,000+ visits to people in need. Nearly 50,000 teams have been registered since the program's inception,

6. Animal interactions improve the physical, emotional and psychological lives of those we serve,

## PET PARTNERS DIFFERENCE: LEARN

**L – Lessens the risk** of disease transmission through infection control protocols, grooming guidelines, raw diet restrictions and animal/handler health requirements

**E – Education of handlers**, including continuing education creates the best-prepared volunteers

**A – Animal Welfare** is a priority supported by re-evaluations.  An aging dog with arthritis may no longer enjoy the same physical contact it did a younger age, leading to safety concerns.

**R – Rigor of evaluation process** provides peace of mind that the team is well prepared for therapy work.

**N – Nine Species** registered for therapy work

### CONTACT PET PARTNERS IF YOU HAVE AN INTEREST IN JOINING THE TEAM!
www.petpartners.org
https://www.facebook.com/petsforhealth
Twitter: @pet_partners
T 425-679-5504 | F 425-679-5539

# INDEX

# CURRICULUM VITAE

## Analeah Green, Ph.D.
Howard Beach, NY
analeah.green.phd@gmail.com
www.linkedin.com/in/analeahgreen
https://www.facebook.com/agreenphd

## SUMMARY

Independent Higher Education Professional
Faculty Instructor at Higher Education Institutions
On-Line and On Campus

## TEACHING PHILOSOPHY

My educational philosophy is that any individual; regardless of his/her stage of life has the ability to pursue an education to obtain a degree. This standpoint greatly influences my teaching philosophy. The mixture of traditional and non-traditional students in any academic program requires access to a variety of learning materials to ensure a comprehension level. This can include 'traditional' methods such as textbook chapters, scholarly articles, or use of PowerPoint slides as well as "non-traditional" forms of material delivery including YouTube videos, media clips, or audio recordings (e.g., Jing applications). The adaptation of educational materials is vital in fostering an effective academic environment and being current with available technology.

I am versed in e-college, Blackboard, Adobe

Connect, and Sakai learning platforms, which enables me to engage with students throughout the learning process. I post Announcements on a weekly basis to inform students of course expectations (e.g., due date of a scheduled assignment and how to submit the document). I create and/or post supplemental resources in the classroom to assist them with the material as needed (i.e. documents, PowerPoint slides, Jing recordings/tutorials, podcasts, videos, etc.). In addition, I strive to respond to inquiries (via e-mail and/or 'Ask the Instructor' forum in the classroom) within 24-48 hours. Per discussion question forums, I make an active effort to respond to each student's initial post and subsequent responses pertaining to the assigned discussion question. Based on previous experience, I've found these methods are extremely effective in not only maintaining a social presence in an online academic environment, but also providing encouragement to the online student in obtaining his/her educational goals.

## EDUCATION

- 2013, Doctorate of Philosophy, Human Services / Administration and Leadership, Walden University, Minneapolis, MN
- 2008, Master of Social Work, New York University, New York, NY
- 2006, Bachelor of Arts, Sociology, State University of New York College at Cortland, Cortland, NY

## ACADEMIC EXPERIENCE

Adjunct Professor, Supervising Instructor, Lecturer
May 2011 – Present
Rutgers University

Develop curriculum and programs; provide public policy
(independent SME); develop and deliver weekly lecture
material, undergraduate and graduate level School of
Social Work students. Lead and facilitate class
discussions and group activities for 16-25 students to
enhance learning. Create exams to assess levels of
student comprehension related to course material.
Provide feedback, consultation, and graded assignment
content to ensure student progress.

Adjunct Faculty
May 2011- Present
University of New England

Lead and facilitated discussion board postings on a daily
basis for 20 plus Master of Social Work Online option
students. Provided feedback, consultation, and graded
assignment content to ensure student progress.
Developed and delivered weekly supplemental material
to enhance student learning and received an average
course evaluation of 4.5 out of 5.0.

*Special Projects*: Content administrator and developer
for Research Methods courses. Creator and facilitator for
Supplemental Instruction weekly lecture series

administered using Blackboard Collaborate.

Behavioral Science Facilitator
Jan 2010 - April 2011
Ross University School of Medicine

Facilitated groups of 10-12 medical students for peer-observed patient interviews and provided guidance to improve on clinical skills. Conducted role playing exercises to demonstrate effective assessment taking methods.

## PROFESSIONAL EXPERIENCE

Case Manager
June 2008 - June 2009
Services Now for Adult Persons

Managed a caseload of 100 plus adult clients ages 60 and older; adhered to New York State Department for the Aging (DFTA) program regulations. Conducted in home psychosocial assessments and compiled individualized care plans to meet client needs. Collaborated and monitored service providers with client status every two months. Received certificate of completion for DFTA sponsored eight week case management training.

Per Diem Social
Nov 2008 - June 2009
ORZAC Center for Extended Care and Rehabilitation

Managed a caseload of 6-10 newly admitted patients per day and conducted psychosocial assessments for individual needs. Consulted with interdisciplinary staff to create, implement, and monitor individualized care plans and services provided.

Social Work
Sept 2007 - May 2008
Henry Street Settlement-Vladeck Cares Program

Managed a caseload of four older adults, age 65 and older referred by the Visiting Nurse Services. Engaged and performed psychotherapy approaches for isolation, depression, and bereavement complications. Monitored client progress and consulted with supervisory staff to meet unmet psychological and concrete needs.

Social Work Intern
Sept 2007 - May 2008
New York Academy of Medicine: Social Work Leadership Institute

Actively participated in the nationwide Hartford Partnership Program for Aging Education (HPPAE) policy initiative through research, evaluation, and networking events. Approved two grant proposals to implement aging-focused social work programs and consulted with program directors of submissions in need of revisions. Prepared and presented at the National Association of Social Workers annual conference on behalf of the program.

Teen Center Coordinator
June 2006 - Aug 2008
The YMCA of Greater New York

Planned and executed weekly activities for youth ages 13-19 with a weekly attendance of 25-40 individuals. Oversaw and delegated tasks to a staff of 10 to promote safety and efficiency within the program. Maintained and compiled weekly documentation to be used for annual grant renewal and executive office reports.

Summer Program Administration
The YMCA of Greater New York

Managed over 100 staff files for payroll procedures and assisted senior program director in executing daily activities for approximately 600 youth ages 5-15. Created and maintained billing spreadsheets for hundreds of third party payments from 1199 Union, Transit Workers Union (TWU), and Administration of Children's Services (ACS) at end of term.

Social Work Intern
Sept 2006 – May 2007
Creedmoor Psychiatric Center Intensive Case Management

Managed a weekly caseload of four high-risk, dual diagnosed chronically and mentally ill adults and provided individual psychotherapy sessions, crisis intervention, and concrete services. Created and distributed a comprehensive Consumer Resource

Manual to 30 staff members. Co-facilitated the monthly Vocational Support Group of approximately 12 patients and participated in the quarterly Consumer Advisory Council to monitor patients discharged into the community.

## LICENSE

New York, Licensed Master of Social Work - #078309

## PRESENTATIONS

Ho, A. (2008). *Progress in social work education: Generating a workforce for older adults*
A poster presentation for the National Association of Social Workers Power of Social Work conference.
Green, A. (2013). *An exploration of transitioning registered handler-animal therapy from the institution to the community.* A 30-minute podium style presentation for the International Veterinary Social Work Summit, University of Tennessee at Knoxville.

## ABOUT THE AUTHOR

**Analeah Green** holds a Ph.D. in Human Services – Administration and Leadership from Walden University, a Master of Social Work (MSW) from New York University, and a Bachelor of Arts in Sociology from the State University of New York College at Cortland. She is a Licensed Master Social Worker (LMSW) in New York State.

Her professional interests include animal-assisted therapy, gerontology, family and caregiver services, staff and program development, grant writing, continuing education, and curriculum development.

Dr. Green is a higher education instructor with

clinical and policy oriented professional experience. With a background in social work, she has worked in a case management capacity assessing and providing concrete services to a range of client populations.

She has interests in gerontology/aging and continuing education, and has incorporated her direct social service experience into traditional and distance learning environments. She is versed in e-College, Blackboard, Adobe Connect, and Sakai platforms, and facilitates courses and creates supplemental material to enhance student learning.

Dr. Green is a Licensed Master Social Worker in New York State and is an integral member within the various forms of higher education (i.e. land-based, hybrid, as well as asynchronous and synchronous online learning platforms) and professional associations.

She welcomes invitations to connect through LinkedIn or can be reached at analeah.green.phd@gmail.com.

**Connect to Dr. Green via LinkedIn:**
www.linkedin.com/in/analeahgreen

Facebook Business Page:
https://www.facebook.com/agreenphd

## ABOUT THE BOOK

If you are familiar with the animal assisted therapy field, you know how important animals can be to people in emotional, physical, or psychological distress. Do you know there is a deficit in programs using animals to increase the productive results of other therapies? Art, musical, physical, and psychological therapists can use animal-assisted activities as a partner therapy for treatment of conditions.

This book focuses on a study that determined the increased positive results of care planning processes and service provision to clients. Interviews with animal-assisted handlers' on their observations of the value of animals in programs that focus on caring for patients or clients in multiple physical and mental health environments are showcased. This book can be a resource to caregivers and families, community-based case management organizations, administrators, and human service professionals.

Read the book to learn more about the challenges and perspectives in the animal-assisted therapy industry.

# D. Boyer Consulting, Virginia Beach, VA 23464
http://dboyerconsulting.com /
Dawn@DBoyerConsulting.com

## Editing, formatting, cover art, and publication
D. Boyer Consulting
www.DBoyerConsulting.com
Virginia Beach, VA
Dawn.Boyer@DBoyerConsulting.com

KEY WORDS: adult day centers, age in place, aging friendly communities, Alzheimer's, Animal Handler, animal therapy programs, Animal-Assisted Therapy (AAT), benefits, bonding social capital, calming effects, canine / dog, caregivers, case management, case study, cat, catalyst, children, clients / patients, clinical practice, clinical professional, coding, cognitive functioning, collective conscience, community-based organizations, companion pets, counseling/counselors, data, demographics, depression, descriptive statistics, disability, domesticated animals, elderly / elders, emotional, empirical phenomenological study, environments, ethnography, experiences, Gemeinschaft, geriatrics, Gesellschaft, grounded theory, healing, home services, homogeneity, hospice/hospital, human service professionals, human-companion, in-patient, Institutional Review Board (IRB), instructor, isolation, interventions, learning disabilities, lived experiences, loneliness, mechanical solidarity, Medicaid, medical care, mental health, methodology, model of care, natural aging process, naturally occurring retirement communities (NORC), nursing facilities, nutritional services, observation, occupational therapist (OT), older adult, Older Americans Act (OAA), Oldest old adults, Olmstead Decision, OnLok, ordinal scale, organic solidarity, out-patient, person-environment, pet ownership, phenomenological design, physical activity, physical therapist (PT), physical touch, prisons, private schools, Program of All-Inclusive Care for the Elderly (PACE), progressive socialization, psychological, psychosocial, psychotherapy, qualitative technique, quantitative technique, raw data, recreational therapist, registered handlers, respite, retirement communities, schools, screening, self-worth, senior centers, sense of purpose, social capital, social service programs, social workers, socialization, solitude, special needs, staff development, stress relief, tactile interaction, talk therapy, therapeutic environment, therapists, therapy animal, Title II of the American Disabilities Act (ADA), volunteers, well-being, wheelchair

www.ingramcontent.com/pod-product-compliance
Lightning Source LLC
Chambersburg PA
CBHW070636290526
45790CB00001B/109